EMILY HAYNES

AMERICAN
GODS

FOREWORD: INTERVIEW WITH
NEIL GAIMAN

Library of Congress Cataloging-in-Publication Data available.

ISBN: 978-1-4521-5605-7
Manufactured in China

MIX
Paper from
responsible sources
FSC™ C104723

Design by Jacob Covey

10 9 8 7 6 5 4 3 2 1

Chronicle books and gifts are available at special quantity
discounts to corporations, professional associations,
literacy programs, and other organizations. For details and
discount information, please contact our corporate/premiums
department at corporatesales@chroniclebooks.com or at
1-800-759-0190.

Chronicle Books LLC
680 Second Street
San Francisco, California 94107
www.chroniclebooks.com

CONTENTS

Foreword

Interview with
Neil Gaiman

In conversation with Emily Haynes

What was the original inspiration for writing American Gods?

NEIL: The original inspiration for writing *American Gods* was moving from the U.K. to America. I was an innocent and I thought because I'd been to America on many occasions—and I'd also written about America and spent my life watching American TV and movies—I thought that I understood America. And then I moved out here and it was so much weirder than I had imagined. I moved to Wisconsin, where it is very cold in the winter, and so many things were strange to me. I began turning to people and saying, "Don't you think this is weird?" And they would say, "No, this is just how you do things." Then I'd say, "Look, this thing where you guys park a car on a frozen lake every year and then take bets for charity about when it's going to fall through the ice—do you think that's weird?" And they'd go, "No, that's just what we do, everybody does this." Then I'd pass signs for things like House on the Rock and think, "Well, I have to go see the House on the Rock." But I'd discover they put up signs advertising it 300 miles away from where it actually is, so now I'm traveling 300 miles to follow up my curiosity about the road sign. I would drive a long way and get to these places and sometimes I'd go, "Ah, I really understand you." And sometimes I'd go, "You are the weirdest place in the world." Out of all of those places, my favorite was really House on the Rock because that really is the weirdest place in the world.

What makes the House on the Rock so strange?

The funny thing about the House on the Rock: I ended up toning it down for the book because nobody would have believed the reality. Season 2 is going to begin in the House on the Rock. People will actually get to see just how weird this place is. It's not just that it has the biggest carousel in the world; it's not just that before you get to the biggest carousel in the world you get to a room with a carousel filled entirely with creepy Victorian dolls; it's not the fact that most of the stuff there is fake, but not everything. I left out the hundred-piece artificial orchestra and the Statue of Liberty in battle with a giant squid with a full-sized boat in its mouth. I wound up editing a lot of it out, thinking people would not believe me.

That's sort of where it began: I'm living in America, there is weird stuff here, I want to do something with it.

The next thing that happened is I started thinking about two people meeting on a plane. It was sort of a weird scenario I'd run through my head before I went to sleep each night, and all I knew was that there are two men meeting on a plane—one older, one younger. One of them winds up getting on the plane—he shouldn't even be on that plane, he definitely shouldn't have been bounced up to first-class. And then when he sits down in first-class, an old guy sitting next to him says, "You're late and I'm offering you a job." I thought, I don't know who these men are, but I'd think about them. One of them felt like he'd just got out of prison and one of them was some kind of wizard or con man or something, but I wasn't even sure what. And now a lot of the weird stuff that I'd been thinking about America is starting to accrete around them, like cosmic debris starting to form a planet. It's not yet a planet, it's just debris, but it's all orbiting together. And then in the summer of the very late nineties, I needed to go to Norway and my travel agent said to me, "If you're going to Norway, did you know that if you fly via Iceland, they will give you a free stopover?" I didn't know that. It's still true—Icelandair loves to encourage people to stop in Reykjavik and spend tourist dollars. I said, "That's a good thing to know. I'd be delighted to. Give me a stopover, I've always wanted to go to Iceland."

At the time, I was living very near Minneapolis. So I get on a plane, which leaves for Iceland at 7:30 at night. I'm wide awake. It lands at 12:30 a.m. Minneapolis time, which is 6:30 in the morning Iceland time. I'm still awake. I think, "Well, I'll just keep going until it gets dark." But it's like the 3rd of July, which means it doesn't get dark. It's three o'clock in the morning, it looks like the sun's gone behind the clouds, and at four o'clock in the morning it looks like full daylight again. My hotel room does not come with anything fancy like dark curtains. So I lie there awake. And the next day, it's Sunday

and I head out in this weird sleepless state and everything is closed. Finally, I found the downtown tourist information place. I wandered in and there was this diorama showing the voyages of Leif Eriksson, and you could see here's the people coming to Iceland, here's the route from Iceland to Greenland, and here's the route from Greenland to Newfoundland, and this is where they would have built their little bases. Then they went home again. And I remember looking at this and thinking, I wonder if they brought their gods with them. Then thinking, I wonder if they left them behind when they went home.

I combined that question with a weird idea I had while writing a comic book called *The Sandman*—in the last *Sandman* story there was a speech I'd had Loki, a Norse god, make about how there are new gods coming, gods of hospitals and freeways, gods of cell phones. And I thought, Oh, there. All of these weird, strange things. This is a book. And it felt lovely, it felt like a book, which was important for me. Also, it felt like the kind of book that would relieve my frustration, because I'd just spent a couple of years doing nothing but film scripts; and the problem with writing film scripts is they're 120 pages long. They have a beginning, a middle, and an end, and they have acts, and they have structure. What I loved about this idea in my head was that it was big and weird. And it

wasn't going to have a beginning, middle, and end—or it would, but it might have several beginnings, and lots of middles, some false ends and some real ends. It was going to be a road story, and it was going to be about all of the things I'd thought about America at the time and all of the things I could see on the horizon.

I got up at around four o'clock the next morning and flew to Oslo, Norway. I was put up in the Grand Hotel in Oslo, where they have these amazing dark curtains that close, and I got two full nights' sleep. Then I sat down in the hotel room and I wrote a description of a book. I don't think Shadow had a name at that point, but I described the book and I got to the end and I said, "It'll have a working title of *American Gods*, but I'll come up with something better." Jennifer Hershey, who was my lovely editor, read the description and got very enthusiastic about the title. And to talk me out of finding something better, she mocked up a beautiful cover. When I got back to America, a color photocopy arrived of a green cover with a road and lightning strike and it said, "*American Gods*. Neil Gaiman." And I said, "Oh, this is my book. And my book cover." It's rather intimidating to have your book cover before you write the book, but there it is. It was nice because it meant that all through the writing process, I had the book cover in front of me. I'd go, "Is this the cover of what I'm writing

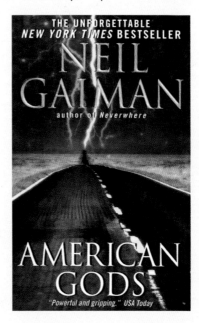

right now? Does it fit underneath that cover?" And occasionally, it was a no and I had to remove it.

I then started writing the book. I wrote chapter 1 in the first person and it didn't really work because you were all the way in Shadow's head. I redid it in third person and it felt like a real thing. Eventually I rented a little log cabin on the lake—much like the one that I give Shadow in the book. I took a mighty oath that I wouldn't get a haircut or shave my beard until the book was done, which meant that roundabout October, I was being mistaken for a homeless person. I quickly finished the first draft, though once I shaved off my beard I was mistaken for Howard Stern. In response to my second draft, Jennifer wrote saying, "This is much, much, much too long. Can we take out all the *Coming to America* stuff and all the weird little digressions to make it a rollicking, powerful thing." And I said, "No. No, we can't do that." But we negotiated and compromised, which meant that the first version of the book that came out was shorter than the tenth-anniversary edition, when I got to bring out the full-length version, the director's cut.

It was published on June 19, 2001. I did a signing for it on the 19th at Borders Books in the World Trade Center. Which seems now, looking back on it, ominous in all possible ways. It made it into the lower reaches of the *New York Times* Best Sellers list.

I think it got the smallest, most perfunctory *New York Times* book review, sort of more or less this-thing-exists review. But it was slowly finding its people. I did a very long signing tour for it. It ended in September and by the time I got home, like two days later the World Trade Center no longer existed, nor did the Borders Books I'd done that signing in. And weirdly, my book, instead of feeling suddenly dated, felt almost more timely.

How did your fans and readers react to the book?

When *American Gods* came out it was gloriously divisive, which I hadn't expected. Five people would love it, four people quite liked it, and two people would really hate it. The latter group didn't like anything about the book, didn't like the way it was written, argued with the philosophy, thought it was boring, thought it was this or that. I found this interesting. There were things I'd done when I wrote the book that I figured would be useful for people who didn't like the book, as a sort of a get-out-early clause. The fifteenth word of the book is "fuck." The Bilquis sex scene occurs at the end of chapter 1. If you can't cope with the language, you know on the third page you can stop. If you cannot cope with the mind-fucking extreme weird magicky sexy thing, it's okay. Stop now and get out early. And it's funny because I feel like that attitude wound up creeping into the finished version of episode 1 of the series. It's gorier and weirder and much more extreme than pretty much anything else in the first series.

How did the book end up being developed for television?

In the years after it was published, I would get phone calls from famous directors I had heard of, and it was the same phone call about four or five times. It would go, "Hello, Neil. I'm a famous director you've actually heard of. I have read *American Gods* and I love it very much. I picked it up at an airport and it blew my mind. I want to make a movie of it. So I have a couple of questions for you." And I'd say, "Great, what are the questions?" And they'd go, "Well, how would you go about turning this into a film, because I'm not really sure how you could do it." And I'd go, "I have no idea. If I had known how to write it as a film, I would have made it film-shaped. As it is, it's almost intentionally not film-shaped. It's big and it's bulbous, and anything that you do to make it film-shaped is going to stop it from being *American Gods*." And they'd go, "Yeah, that's what I thought." And that would be the last I'd hear of it. And then, TV started changing. The DVD, binge-watching, all of that just changed what television is. There was an executive at Playtone, Tom Hanks's company, named Stefanie Berk. She loved the project and really believed in it—she pushed and pushed to do it at HBO. But it became obvious that it was not going to happen there, and then Stefanie left for someplace called Fremantle. As the rights came back to me, Stefanie got in touch and said, "Are you still up for working with me because I have absolute faith in this?" And I said, "Yes, I think you're awesome. You've never been anything less than sensible, supportive, and absolutely a part of this." So Stefanie and I met up in LA and she introduced me to Craig Cegielski from Fremantle, a mysterious figure who

is either incredibly good at what he does or he has terrifying, godlike powers and should be stoned or pushed from a mountaintop. We decided he was just very good at what he does. So Craig, Stefanie, and I became a little three-man show. But we knew we needed to find a writer as well as a showrunner who was also a really good writer.

On the first of April 2014, we flew to Toronto and met Bryan Fuller. I flew out from Woodstock, NY, Stefanie flew out from LA, and we sat and had a long chat with him about *American Gods*, what it was, why it was. He was a fan who was intimidated in the right way by the material. His attitude was, "I love the book. I never thought it would be possible to make it into a TV series. I'm not sure how you do it, but

I'm really intrigued." And that's where things began. A year later, he and Michael Green were writing scripts and a year after that, David Slade was shouting, "Action!" in Toronto.

Given the book's passionate fan base, is there something you're excited to be giving them with the series that they can't get in the book?

I couldn't have written a version of the book that was three times as long. But I always wanted to go and follow Laura around. I tried to do a thing where you're following Shadow's story, but you know there are lots of other stories going on, and these are the stories that have a life of their own. Yes, here's Bilquis's story, here's Technical Boy's story arc, here's Laura, here's Mad Sweeney. You're basically getting their stories

SC 137 - 1

SC 137 - 2

SC 137 - 3

SC 137 - 4A

SC 137 - 4B

SC 137 - 5

SC 137 - 6A

SC 137 - 6B

SC 137 - 6C

SC 137 - 6D

SC 137 - 6E

SC 137 - 6F

SC 137 - 6G

SC 137 - 6H

**AMERICAN GODS - THE BONE ORCHARD
DRIVING SEQUENCE - SC 137**

as Shadow encounters them and every now and then I let myself just nip out and give you a little bit of something that isn't Shadow's story. Here's a little bit of Bilquis, a little bit of Sam Black Crow, and Laura, but fundamentally it's Shadow's story and that's whose head you're in. The joy of television is we're not stuck just following Shadow anymore. Shadow and Wednesday are the heart of the show, but now we get to find out what Laura and Mad Sweeney and the rest were doing when the book wasn't looking at them. And I love that we get to do that.

Do you see that as changing what was in the book or just filling in the scenes that you couldn't see?

Sometimes we've changed stuff. A lot of the time, we've filled stuff in. It feels like we're buttressing it. In the book it's as if we got to walk into this big house and explore the downstairs. Now we're walking around the downstairs, and the upstairs, and we're stepping out into the gardens. And you're going, "Oh! This is bigger and stranger than I thought it was." And it's still the same house. We may have repainted a few rooms and redecorated a few things, but it's the same house.

Did you come across any challenges going from the internal narrative of the book to the visual storytelling of television?

One of the joys of working with Bryan Fuller and Michael Green is that they've taken the impossible and made it happen. There are sequences you can write in a book where you go, "This is a book scene. Nobody is ever going to be able to do this on-screen. Look, I just had a guy meet a taxi driver who is a genie and they've gone off to his hotel room and they're having jinn sex. A mortal man and a fire creature, and now he's ejaculating flame inside him." This is the kind of thing you're never going to be able to put on-screen, and then they send you the script and you go, "I was wrong about that. You *can* put that in a script. You absolutely can." Things like that for me are so remarkable.

Were there moments or characters you were particularly excited to see once you saw the reels?

I think Mad Sweeney. I never expected to fall in love with Mad Sweeney. Pablo Schreiber's performance is just astonishing because, yes, he's saying the same lines he said in the book, but there's so much charm in them you just want to spend more time in his company. I wound up giving Bryan and Michael a history of Mad Sweeney. "Ah, let me give you five thousand years of Mad Sweeney. This is who he was, what he becomes as a god, this is how things work, this is how his downfall happens." Because I want to see more of him. He's wonderful.

How did you decide to expand Laura's role for the series?

It was the nature of the book that everything is from Shadow and Wednesday's perspective. The women in Shadow's life— like the men in Shadow's life except Wednesday—tend to be peripheral. Part of the joy for me of working on the series is that now we can give Laura her due. Seeing how Emily Browning took Laura and just made her feel so real and so complicated was an absolute joy for me.

What does the series add to the conversation about immigration we're having nationally at the moment, and around the world?

That's a great question. I was thrilled to see how much more relevant the material is, how it really feels like it has not become dated. On the other hand, there was a lot of stuff that I put in the novel that I never thought would be in any way contentious. The idea of refugees, the idea that this is a nation of immigrants and you tell it as immigrant stories, the idea of a racially diverse cast, the idea of inspecting with clear eyes the darker sides of America's history. None of that stuff seemed to me to be in any way contentious. The fact is that we've wound up in a world in which these topics are incredibly divisive. We didn't set out to make something that is this politically relevant. The world we live in changed around us. We were just telling our story. †

EMILY HAYNES

INTRODUCTION

WHEN *AMERICAN GODS* WAS first published in 2001, the book garnered immediate acclaim and an ardent fan base. But it would take almost fifteen years for the book to make the jump from page to screen. Other works by Neil Gaiman were adapted in the meantime, including *Coraline* and *Stardust*, and he collaborated on a variety of original and adapted screenplays. While Gaiman's filmography grew over the years, *American Gods* languished in option limbo. Perhaps it was fate that it would take a decade and a half for this sprawling, cinematic, fantastical tale to come to life. It is surprisingly relevant for today's viewers, perhaps even more so than when it was first published.

When the book hit bookstore shelves in June of 2001 the world was a very different place. George W. Bush was president, Google was only three years old, and the Twin Towers still reigned over New York. Understanding the state of the world when *American Gods* was written, and all the technological advances, wars, and political movements we've witnessed since then, underscores how ahead of its time it was. In a pre-9/11 world it examined topics—immigration, technology, religion and faith—that would only grow in prominence, and divisiveness, in American culture (and around the world) after that fateful day.

> "Neil really celebrates America, but he also taps us on the shoulder and says, 'There's a slight hypocrisy to this whole thing.' Bryan and Michael wanted to put a spotlight on it. There's a beautiful poetry between the little moments that make America great and the fact that we are blinded by our own hypocrisy."
>
> —*Craig Cegielski, executive producer*

FROM BOOK TO SCREEN

FAST-FORWARD A DOZEN or so years, and executive producer Stefanie Berk, who had been attempting to get a series based on the book off the ground at HBO for several years, joined Fremantle. Upon her arrival, Craig Cegielski, another executive producer at the company, asked her what her passion project was. "*American Gods,*" she said. After the rights reverted back to Gaiman from HBO, Berk, Cegielski, and Gaiman started the series development again from scratch. Their first challenge was finding the right showrunner for the project. "One of the things that Stefanie and I talked about from the get-go," Cegielski explains, "was to find somebody who was like-minded and had that lyrical, poetic storytelling voice." They interviewed dozens of filmmakers and writers, but were having a hard time finding a person that was not too literal in their approach, someone with ideas that would take the world that Gaiman had created and expand it, give it legs and see what it might become. Then they reached out to Bryan Fuller, who had developed a diverse filmography over the last decade, including *Dead Like Me*, *Pushing Daisies*, and *Hannibal*. It was clear from their first call that they had found their man.

Soon after he began work on the series Fuller realized that he needed to share the development and writing load. Enter Michael Green, with whom Fuller had worked in the writer's room on *Heroes*. Their collaboration on *American Gods* turns out to be even greater than the sum of their parts. "They're both so good," Stefanie Berk comments. "It's like having the two smartest people in the room working with each other. They really push each other to be their best because the level of respect that they have for each other is so high. It's almost like they are trying to outperform each other creatively."

It can be tricky, though, to work with material that comes from such a beloved author. Thankfully, Gaiman was both a passionate and a flexible collaborator. He didn't need to let go of his work and fear the inevitable changes to character and plot, as is often the case with original creators of literary works that are adapted to the screen. Gaiman saw the series as an opportunity to expand the material in ways he couldn't in the book. He had always wondered what the characters got up to between scenes, what their backstories might be; but the book needed to remain in Shadow's point of view to keep a central thread in an already sprawling narrative. The show gave him the keys to a world he had already built, with doors he'd not yet been able to open.

Gaiman was intimately involved in the development process and reviewing the dailies—the first prints from a scene made for quick review by the director and writer—though he gave the driving creative freedom over to Fuller and Green. While conflicts occasionally came up, the process was also collaborative and empowering. "We gave Neil outlines, scripts, and cuts of episodes," Fuller explains. "Sometimes when we'd be breaking story and staring at a dry-erase board, we'd call him and say, 'What do you think of this?' We argued most heatedly about the smallest of details. But our disagreements almost always led to a third option that we all liked better."

COMING TO AMERICA

IMMIGRATION TOPPED THE list of themes that Fuller, Green, and Gaiman wanted to explore in the series. If there is a single larger story running through *American Gods*, it is the tale of how various peoples came to land on these shores, and the things, ideas, and gods they brought with them. What survives and what declines in the melting pot of America, and the casualties that pile up along the way, is the story of our country, a narrative that each generation faces anew. This theme makes a group of fantastical characters, from Mad Sweeney to Anubis, human and relatable. Most Americans have relatives they can point to who emigrated from another country, whether it's a first-generation Indian American motel owner, or a great-great-grandmother who escaped poverty in Ireland or persecution in Eastern Europe. Many others can trace their American story back to an ancestor who did not come here by choice, having been brought over in the bowels of a slave ship. As new arrivals fought to survive, culturally and economically, in this new land, they each saw their traditions and beliefs diluted as subsequent generations assimilated into the dominant culture of the time.

THIS THEME IS explored in a recurring element of the show: the *Coming to America* vignettes. From the arrival of Odin with a group of Vikings in the ninth century, to the story of the Queen of Sheba escaping Iran on a plane to Hollywood in the 1970s, these are imaginative pieces of backstory showing how, and why, these once powerful gods ended up on American soil. While the particulars of their experiences and conflicts are magnified, given their powers and the heightened stakes,

"When Neil Gaiman was driving across America writing the book, he was fascinated by the middle of the country, where there are some very divergent viewpoints. What is it to look at those issues through a neutral character's point of view? Which of course in this case is Shadow Moon."
—*Adam Kane, executive producer and director of episodes 6 and 7*

their struggles to fit in and find relevance within American culture would be familiar to any first-generation transplant. "What makes the *Coming to America*s so memorable is that we go inside someone's personal immigration story," Green elaborates. "We get a sense, both literally and figuratively, of what was in their pockets. They brought with them a culture, songs, books, memories, and beliefs. When they closed their eyes to pray for something they needed in this new world, who did they pray to? In the wonderful world of *American Gods,* if people believe it, they manifest it, whether it was six hundred years ago, or just this morning."

"Before I read the book again, I sat down and wrote a quick list of everything I remembered from reading it eleven years earlier. Two things surprised me. One: how much I remembered. Not because my memory is so special, but because the book is so indelible. Two: that at the top of my list were all the *Coming to America* stories. I think they stuck in my mind because every American has a family lore of how they came here, the legend of their last name."

—*Michael Green, executive producer*

A MATTER OF FAITH

THE UNITED STATES is a predominantly Christian nation, with almost 70 percent of the adult population identifying as either Protestant or Catholic. All other faiths—Islam, Hinduism, Judaism, etc.—make up just 7 percent. The balance is filled out by the agnostics, atheists, and the nonreligious. So it might strike readers as a bit odd that, in the book, Gaiman makes no mention of Jesus. This omission was purposeful—he felt that Jesus had no hand to play in the turf battle between the Old and New Gods. He existed above the fray, the penthouse tenant of a luxury high-rise towering over a turf war going on in the streets below. He might be aware of the strife on the streets in a general sense, but would likely pass over and through it as if it were so much scenery.

That is not to say that Gaiman didn't consider adding Jesus to the book. He sketched out some ideas, but a novel only gives the writer so much real estate, and *American Gods* was already on the long side. The series, however, had no such constraints. As a visual medium, it could move much faster than the book, efficiently establishing scenes and characters. While the bulk of the first season is spent introducing the Old and New Gods from the book (plus a few others), the filmmakers felt that it was important, given the opportunity, to include Jesus in this depiction of faith in America. In one of the series' largest plot departures, he appears at Easter's mansion in the final episode of season 1, though not as the individual, omniscient, all-powerful figure most would expect. "The idea we hit on," Green explains, "was that rather than perceiving Jesus as a trinity, we could imagine him as a multiplicity to represent the many different types of worshippers. The Jesuses may have different skin colors, or different mannerisms, different regalia. That is not to say that Jesus is from a polytheistic religion, but rather that being a Christian can mean many different things."

This sensitive and inventive treatment of religion is typical for Green and Fuller's approach to the material. Both come from a religious background—Fuller was raised Catholic and Green Jewish—and their personal journeys through faith gave them a perspective and knowledge base to write from. Some might assume that a series like *American Gods*, which takes great liberty with sex and violence, would be similarly sensational and flippant about religion. But Green and Fuller took the subject, and the responsibility of representing the diversity of faiths in America, quite seriously. "There's an incorrect assumption that anytime anyone from the entertainment industry touches on religion, they're going to be cynical and negative," comments Green. "That was never our approach. We came at it from a place of fascination and reverence. The adaption of the book felt like a way to celebrate it, to explore what having faith means in America today. *American Gods* allows us to level the playing field and suggest that everyone's faith has an equal level of reality and is worth probing."

The differences in their religious upbringings also informed their writing. For Fuller, his experience of Catholicism was complicated by the fact that while his mother was devout, his father was an atheist. "My father would mock my mother for taking the children to church," Fuller explains, "which created this early awareness that not everyone believes the same thing. Traditionally, in a household, there is a homogeneity of beliefs, but we were raised with an ongoing discourse on how to approach faith."

"The book is based on the notion of thought-form, which is that if you believe in something enough, and enough people believe, you can manifest what you believe into reality. You believe Jesus Christ into being because you have faith in Him. You believe Buddha into being, because you have so much faith in him. This applies not only to gods, but also demigods, and lesser supernatural folks, like leprechauns. It can extend into certain urban legends, and we're excited about delving into different aspects of cultural beliefs in season 2, that we weren't able to explore in season 1."
—*Bryan Fuller, executive producer*

When Fuller started talking to Green about their backgrounds, he realized that Green had experienced his faith differently. Rather than the punitive Catholic approach to theology, which instilled in Fuller lessons about what you needed to learn and do to avoid burning in hell for all eternity, Judaism immersed Green in the joy of storytelling and metaphor as a way of understanding the world. "For Michael, religious mythologies were conveyed as though they were J.R.R. Tolkien," Fuller explains. "There was a joy in the storytelling that he could learn from abstractly. If I had been given the delivery mechanism of a wonderful story to absorb theological points of view, I would have had a different experience."

American Gods gives both showrunners a chance to flex that storytelling muscle, and explore what having faith means in America today. While they come from Judeo-Christian backgrounds, the show provides a level playing field, giving voice to the ancient, the mythological, and the modern theologies and mythologies. Though the show does away with the idea of a

"You are pretending you cannot believe in impossible things."

—MR. WEDNESDAY,

EPISODE 3

religious monopoly in which one god is invalid because of the existence of another, it moves another tribal war to the forefront in its place. This war is between the gods and the modern world, with each side applying many of those tried and true religious psychological tricks of dogma and devotion to gain the upper hand. "There's a tribalism instinct in our lizard brains, that there is safety in numbers," Fuller explains. "We attract like-minded folks and then warn them of what happens if they think differently. Both sides—New and Old Gods—use these political ploys to curry favor with their believers and amass a movement against the perceived enemy."

THESE THEMES OF *American Gods*—immigration and faith—have been defining questions of identity and belonging ever since the first migration of man out of Africa 1.5 million years ago. There is no end to the conflicts that arise when someone perceived as an "other" arrives in a new land, sending cultural ripples through society. People will always fight, and they will always adapt, until the next generation comes along. But even as new conflicts arise, our society moves ever forward on that grand moral arc of the universe, inching toward equality and justice. Just as the book was written in a pre-9/11 world, and proved all the more relevant in the wake of those events, the series was produced before the 2016 presidential election, which put the level playing field of the gods that Gaiman created in a whole new context. In the wake of the election there have been protests, debates, hate crimes, acts of war, and policy reversals centered around those central themes. Into this raw wound of American identity comes *American Gods*. It asks us to listen to the stories of those around us. To consider the relevance of all peoples, regardless of faith, hue, creed, or origin. And to realize the price we will pay in the coming war—of our values, our identities, and our selves—if we do not heed the lessons of the past. †

PART ONE

DO YOU BELIEVE

?

SHADOW MOON

IN ANYONE'S CONVERSION, IT HELPS
TO MEET A GOD ON AN AIRPLANE.

— MICHAEL GREEN, EXECUTIVE PRODUCER

WHO IS SHADOW MOON? Is he a con man? A prisoner? A sacrificial lamb? A hero? A believer? These questions arise from the first moment we meet Shadow in his jail cell, where he anticipates his pending release and his reunion with the love of his life, Laura. Yet his dreams are immediately dashed on the rocks of the warden's revelation: His wife has just died in a car crash in the early hours of the morning. Even before Shadow walks out of the prison gates, he is revealed as an internal, introverted man, one who keenly observes the world while riding out the tempests that are thrown at him.

Rather than restarting his life with Laura, Shadow flies home for her funeral. On the plane ride, he meets Mr. Wednesday, a strangely persistent man who makes him an offer: to become Wednesday's bodyguard. If Laura were alive, Shadow might easily dismiss this request, but she is not. Instead, Mr. Wednesday's odd words sink through the cracks in Shadow's psyche, and he says yes, setting in motion a journey into faith, fear, and the heart of America.

"Shadow is a broken man," says actor Ricky Whittle, who plays Shadow Moon. "His wife died on the eve of his release. The one thing he had in the world has betrayed him. This betrayal leaves Shadow broken and damaged." As Whittle explains, Shadow's name has metaphorical significance: "When we meet him, he's a shadow of his former self. But he's also a shadow of who he's about to become. Through Mr. Wednesday and the fantastical journey of theirs, he starts an evolution from cynic to believer."

The series *American Gods* imagines a world populated by gods, the undead, and a lanky leprechaun, among many other mythical and magical beings, and it throws into the middle of them an "average American," as executive producer Michael Green describes Shadow. Human and relatable, Shadow is thrust headfirst into a series of astonishing events—miraculous, godly, and human—that challenge his lack of religious belief. In doing so, the story asks, "What would you believe if this happened to you? What is your breaking point between reality and faith in the improbable?" When they first meet, Wednesday asks Shadow the same question: "What do you believe?" Understandably, Shadow does not know how to answer.

"When fantastical, beautiful miracles happen in the world," Whittle elaborates, "it's human nature to search for scientific or logical explanations. But what happens when those events pile up, and you can no longer explain them? That's the struggle that Shadow faces. There comes a point where Shadow must start to believe. It's that awakening that makes him into the man he will become."

Through much of season 1, the question is, how long, and how much, will it take for Shadow to believe? Shadow's lack of belief matters because, without belief, he will never be able to sacrifice himself to save Mr. Wednesday. And Wednesday needs him to reach that level of commitment, since Shadow will play an important role in the larger drama that Wednesday is orchestrating. Yet in *American Gods,* the issue of belief is more than a plot device. The story of Shadow's evolution of faith is also a parable about modern humanity's disconnection from the history, culture, and beliefs of our forefathers. Like Shadow,

we no longer believe in the Old Gods of traditional spirituality and ancient mythology. Instead, we have fallen for the seductions of the technological age, as we spend hours each day praying before our devices. Every age believes in something, and these are our New Gods.

"That's the world we live in now," Whittle says about the New Gods. "We've moved away from the biblical and mythical beliefs in faith. You take anyone's mobile phone off them, and they'll lose their minds!"

"SHADOW'S ARC IS ONE OF BECOMING A BELIEVER, A RELIGIOUS JOURNEY. HE'S A NONPASSIONATE AGNOSTIC WHO QUESTIONS HIS OWN COMPLACENCY AND COMES TO A VALID BELIEF IN SOMETHING THAT HE WOULD NEVER HAVE IMAGINED HAVING IMPORTANCE TO HIM PRIOR TO MEETING MR. WEDNESDAY."

: MICHAEL GREEN :
EXECUTIVE PRODUCER

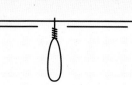

CASTING SHADOW

AMERICAN GODS IS a beloved novel, and fan expectations weighed heavily on the production team as they prepared to bring the story to the screen. Casting the lead role, Shadow Moon, was a particular concern. For months before an announcement was made, casting rumors bounced around Twitter and online, and some fans even suggested Ricky Whittle as an ideal candidate. After reviewing thousands of audition tapes, the casting directors and showrunners came to the same conclusion.

Now considered a perfect fit for Shadow's brooding, thoughtful con artist, Whittle still had to endure an arduous audition process. He recorded sixteen audition tapes over the course of casting. Orly Sitowitz, one of the show's lead casting directors, explains, "Ricky came in and, to his credit, was prepared to do anything he had to do. He read the book a hundred times. He learned how to roll the coins on his fingers; he went to a magician. Before he was cast, he was all in. He was committed, insanely so."

Neil Gaiman's depiction of Shadow in the novel doesn't say much about the character's appearance. We know that his mother is black, that he has gray eyes, and that he's "big enough, and looked don't-fuck-with-me enough" (*American Gods*, chapter 1). Beyond that, readers are left to envision the character for themselves. For the show's producers, however, that meant there was one nonnegotiable when it came to casting Shadow. It was paramount that the actor not be white. The showrunners were relieved that the network, Starz, heartily approved that decision.

"It was tough finding a good location for the hotel where Shadow reunites with his dead wife, because a lot of these great, old motels have been torn down or left to rot. We needed to find something ordinary, but beautiful at the same time. I'd had my eye on this motel that's a bit outside of Toronto—it's a lonely motel at the side of a highway. It ended up working perfectly for our Starbrite motel."

—*Rory Cheyne, production designer*

A NEW SHADOW

FOR MICHAEL GREEN and Bryan Fuller, the co-showrunners, deciding how to embody Shadow's character presented one of their first challenges. Shadow is a small-time con man who has learned to keep his emotions subdued and his reactions in check, and he's been hardened further by years in prison. Yet on-screen, demonstrative performances are the most effective. "Shadow is very internal in the novel," Fuller explains. "We follow what he's thinking because we're reading his thoughts. We debated at the beginning: Should we have a voice-over narration of Shadow to guide him through this? Or do we make his character more proactive, more engaged in his journey? And how do we do that without making him different from who he is in the novel?"

In the end, voice-over didn't feel like a good fit for the show, which follows multiple characters as they arc through the story. To have a voice-over just for Shadow would have thrown the narrative structure out of balance. The showrunners decided they needed to make Shadow more proactive, but without altering him so much that he was unrecognizable to the novel's many fans. "How do we get him to stand up to Wednesday so he doesn't seem like a passenger in the story?" Fuller elaborates. "That works great in the novel because we know exactly what Shadow is thinking, but it doesn't translate to television, where you want to see a character who is taking some agency in their life."

At first, Ricky Whittle struggled to find the right approach for the character. "When I started playing Shadow," he explains, "I was trying to remain true to the book, so I played him very stoic, internal, and quiet. They wanted Shadow to be a bit more colorful, more human, and not so blasé about fantastical things happening."

On-screen, Shadow engages more in the action. He doesn't react like a blank slate; he pushes back. For example, in episode 1, "The Bone Orchard," Shadow first encounters Technical Boy, one of the New Gods, and a conversation and assault ensues that would strike most people as bizarre and deeply unsettling. In the book, when Shadow later confronts Mr. Wednesday about this attack, he remains relatively subdued. After some small talk, Shadow finally reveals that he was hijacked "by a fat kid in a limo" (*American Gods,* chapter 3). In the show, the same scene (which appears in episode 2) is pitched higher emotionally. When they meet, Shadow's first words to Wednesday are: "The fuck—did you do?"

An even more dramatic example is in episode 3, when Shadow's dead wife, Laura, turns up in his hotel room, talking and looking very much undead. "In the book, Shadow is at ease with it and goes with the flow," Whittle recalls. "The book says, 'Living or dead, he couldn't fear her.' That's a beautiful moment. But in real life, as much as I would love a dead relative to return to me, I'm probably going to run a mile and be freaked out."

In the screen version, Shadow is more freaked out than at ease, reflecting Whittle's sense that, whatever attraction and longing drives the character, it would be balanced by a very human impulse to deny the supernatural.

DRESSING SHADOW

COMPARED TO THE more elaborate costumes of the gods on the show, Shadow brings a minimalism to his look that is in line with the subdued, everyman nature of his character. Suttirat Anne Larlarb, the show's much-loved costume designer, sought inspiration both from the book's source material and from other photographers. "There's this photographer who took a bunch of images in prison," she explains, "including this one beautiful silhouette of a prisoner in the prison yard on a hill. It's moody and pensive with not a lot of definition of what he's wearing. To me, that encapsulated Shadow."

> "FOR ME, THE BIGGEST CHALLENGE WAS STOPPING MYSELF FROM BEING SO ATTACHED TO THE BOOK. ALTHOUGH WE'RE STAYING TRUE TO THE STORY LINES AND CHARACTERS, WE HAVE TO UNLEASH THE SHACKLES A BIT TO LET OUR LEGS RUN FASTER THAN WE WOULD IN THE BOOK. IT WAS A BALANCING ACT BETWEEN TV AND STAYING TRUE TO WHAT THE FANS KNOW AND LOVE."
>
> : RICKY WHITTLE :

Early in season 1, Shadow's character is defined by his internal nature and lack of self-knowledge, especially as he struggles to accept what's happening and understand himself. As such, Larlarb chose monochromatic, nondescript, functional clothing that lacked any overt personality. "It helps that we first meet him in prison," Larlarb says, "so there's not a whole lot of personality that can come through. I used the fact that he was in a uniform to anonymize him at the outset. When we go into his backstory, we pump up certain aspects of his character through his costume."

Not that the costume department didn't have some fun with Shadow. After Shadow's clothes are ruined during his battle with Technical Boy, we next see him in a T-shirt that depicts a red buffalo, a key symbol pulled directly from Shadow's dreams.

SETTING THE TONE

DAVID SLADE, THE director for the first three episodes of *American Gods*, was tasked with developing the tone and palette for the show, which would be carried forward through the entire season by the various episode directors. While each director

brought their own particular set of tools and techniques to their episode, they looked to Slade's work as the foundation for the show's overall color, tone, and perspective.

In episode 1, Slade used Shadow and later Mr. Wednesday to help define the visual experience of the show. He decided from the beginning that the real world and the gods' world would differ in warmth and hue. Shadow's prison world is largely monochromatic and purposely stripped of any bright colors. In contrast, when he meets Mr. Wednesday on the plane, there's a wonderful aura of warmth to the setting and his character.

This effect was achieved both in a practical sense—through the selection of materials and lighting—and through "color timing," a post-production process that creates a palette of color that is applied across the entire show in order to create color continuity. The color timing on *American Gods* was done by Dave Hussey, whom Slade had worked with for fifteen years. "David is an expert in color," Slade comments. "He went frame-by-frame, shot-by-shot, to colorize the image. He sweetened the hue or changed it entirely, adding tones of color and sharpness. A really large part of what makes *American Gods* look the way it looks is down to the color timing—it's very rich. There's nothing that looks like this show."

Another way that Slade's work on episodes 1, 2, and 3 defined the approach of the rest of the show was through

sheer scale and ambition. The first season has sets that range from Edwardian England and colonial America, to the Queen of Sheba's temple, a disco in 1970s Iran, and a nineteenth-century slave ship. Each episode brings a new level of scale and complexity, both in practical sets (built on the soundstage from tangible materials) and effects and in VFX. The VFX producer, Bernice Howes, estimates that about 2,400 shots in the first season include some level of VFX, which is an incredible number for a six-month-long television production.

This tone was set from the opening scene of the series, the Viking voyage *Coming to America* vignette, and continued through the first three episodes as Slade introduces us to Shadow and Wednesday, and their trip across America. "Here's the thing about *American Gods*," Slade elaborates. "It's a massive road movie with visual effects, props, prosthetics, guns, everything you can imagine. No one wanted to do it the easy way. Everyone wanted to do it the best way. So if that meant building a set and a crane to use practical effects for the moment that Shadow looks up to the ceiling in his jail cell and sees Laura, and not doing it with visual effects, which would be quicker and easier, that was the way it had to be. If I look back at the stuff that's turned out the best, it is always the stuff that was the hardest to do."

Starbrite

"I believe the shit out of love."

—SHADOW MOON,
Episode 3

Odin

The first episode of *American Gods*, "The Bone Orchard," opens with the arrival of the Vikings in the year 813 CE on the rocky shores of North America. They wish to plunder and explore this undiscovered land, but they are foiled by a barrage of arrows every time they step toward the waiting tree line. No attempt to come further ashore than the beach is successful, with several Vikings finding their end as more pincushion than warrior. The sailors attempt to retreat, but are stymied by a becalmed sea. It seems that Odin, the unseen but deadly god that they have brought with them from the old country, is not satisfied with their demonstration of devotion, or the lack thereof, and has stranded them on this perilous shore. The bloody negotiation that ensues between the adventurous explorers and their mercurial and exacting ancient god sets the tone for a show that throws mortals, gods, and the undead into a volatile mix.

This scene is the first in a series of *Coming to America* vignettes that are interspersed with the modern-day drama; almost like mini-movies, they illustrate how the Old Gods arrived on this continent. However, executive producers Bryan Fuller and Michael Green had originally planned to open the series with a very different scene: Mrs. Fadil's encounter with Death, in the form of Anubis (which now begins episode 3, "Head Full of Snow"). This softer story, with a more benevolent and equitable god at the helm, would have set a very different tone for the series. But Fuller and Green eventually wanted something with more impact, and they wanted to introduce the Old God, who is Mr. Wednesday. But since Odin does not actually appear in person in the Viking vignette, the connection between Odin and Mr. Wednesday would only be known to those already familiar with the book.

"When we started moving the *Coming to America* stories around," Fuller explains, "we looked at what was going to provide the best topic sentence for each episode." Odin, it turns out, is a great topic sentence for the entire series. Even Mr. Wednesday's name draws from Odin's mythology. In Old English, the word for Wednesday is *Wōdnesdæg*, meaning the day of the Germanic god Wōden, who was known as Odin among northern Germanic peoples. The brutality and mean-spirited playfulness Odin displays in his interaction with the Vikings may be tempered a bit in modern times, but as Mr. Wednesday, Odin still packs a wicked punch.

"They were hungry, of course, having made their way through their stores of dried meat and salt fish days ago, even though carefully, professionally rationed. To a man they were expert seamen. Yet no expertise can surmount a sea that does not wish you to reach shore."

—Mr. Ibis, episode 1

MR. WEDNESDAY

> **"WEDNESDAY IS A SHIT-STARTER TO THE BONE. IF YOUR INTENTION IS TO REST AND BE COMFORTABLE, THEN WEDNESDAY IS UNWELCOME NEWS."**
> —MICHAEL GREEN, EXECUTIVE PRODUCER

ODIN, THE BRUTAL GOD of war depicted in the first episode's *Coming to America* vignette, is a far cry from the god Shadow meets on the plane ride home for Laura's funeral. Viewers are forced to wonder: What happened to the god who stranded his devotees on treacherous shores if they dared embark on a mission without paying proper tribute in blood? How could that awesome force, which once ruled over much of northern Europe, now be Mr. Wednesday, a con man tricking a confused ticket agent into upgrading him to first-class?

Though still a force to be reckoned with, Mr. Wednesday embodies the decline of the Old Gods from the height of their power. Once all-powerful as the revered Norse god of war, death, and knowledge, this modern-day Odin plays with a lesser arsenal of tricks and tools, as he manipulates and plots his way toward one final battle of New Gods against Old. Still, though a man of his times, Mr. Wednesday is not one to be trifled with. "Wednesday is a mixture of human and godly qualities, not all of which can be described as good," says actor Ian McShane, who plays Mr. Wednesday. "But I liked that, the fact that he's got his capricious, wicked side, but he believes he's in the right."

Ricky Whittle, who plays Shadow, concurs: "Mr. Wednesday is a devious and sneaky man. He's very good at manipulation. The New Gods could have taken some pointers from him."

As those New Gods soon discover, they just may have met their match in this road-tripping pair, who crisscross America recruiting a motley crew of Old Gods to their cause. Our understanding of Mr. Wednesday's power grows as we come to understand the scope of his manipulation of the unsuspecting Shadow, which began long before Shadow stepped out of the prison gates. As Whittle explains: "Mr. Wednesday is very clever not to actually say, 'Hey, look. I'm this, I'm that, and this is how the world is.' Wednesday places evidence in front of Shadow and wants him to make decisions for himself and come to his own conclusions."

"MR. WEDNESDAY IS A NAUGHTY AND APPEALING SMALL-TIME CON MAN, RATHER ELEGANTLY DRESSED, SMART, BRIGHT, AND WANDERING ACROSS AMERICA. HE PLEASES HIMSELF, HAS A GOOD TIME, AND DOES EXACTLY WHAT HE WANTS WHEN YOU MEET HIM."

: IAN McSHANE :

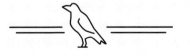

WHAT DO YOU BELIEVE?

MANIFESTATIONS OF FAITH permeate *American Gods*. What one believes matters, since beliefs become manifest. Slavish devotion to the powers of technology have yielded the New Gods, which wield control over humanity's psyche, while those who nurture their faith in their culture's religious roots might be granted an unseen hand of protection by the god of their childhood. For Mr. Wednesday, the question "What do you believe?" is more than academic. It matters because without belief he and the other gods might cease to exist. And it matters specifically in his relationship with Shadow. Mr. Wednesday needs Shadow to complete that leap of faith to fulfill his potential. Without belief, Shadow is just a man, a driver, a helper, and a fighter. With belief, he can become a partner in the war against the New

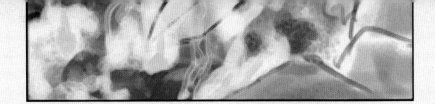

Gods. During the first season, Wednesday repeatedly poses this question to Shadow, pressing him to dig deep for an authentic answer: Do you believe in me? The answer Wednesday wants is a long time coming.

"Shadow doesn't know what to believe," McShane explains. "He suffers from the frustration of the faithless. Wednesday sums it up in one of the key lines of the show: 'If you don't believe in anything, you'll be hard-pressed to back up anything.' But belief in God, Buddha, whatever your faith is, that will make your god believe in you, and the whole world will be a little better."

As mystical events pile up, Shadow's crisis of faith—or of nonfaith, in his case—increases. Finally, in episode 3, during a bank heist, Mr. Wednesday asks Shadow to make it snow. Shadow seems almost amused by the task. He half-heartedly indulges the request, and this is enough to let a little faith into his being. The snow comes—improbable, beautiful, blanketing white snow. Shadow unleashes a hint of his potential power, and he must confront the fact that, somehow, he really did create snow. Nevertheless, as with everything else, Wednesday takes this triumph in stride. Bigger challenges await, and they must keep moving.

THE COAT MAKES THE MAN

IN CHAPTER 1 of the novel *American Gods*, Neil Gaiman introduces Mr. Wednesday with a vivid physical description: "His hair was a reddish-gray; his beard, little more than stubble, was grayish-red. He was smaller than Shadow, but he seemed to take up a hell of a lot of room. A craggy, square face with pale gray eyes. The suit looked expensive, and was the color of melted vanilla ice cream. His tie was dark gray silk, and the tiepin was a tree, worked in silver: trunk, branches, and deep roots."

Actor Ian McShane certainly possesses the gravitas that Mr. Wednesday requires, though not the reddish-gray hair and beard. Instead, in the series, McShane's wavy black hair and rugged but clean-shaven face define Wednesday, along with that vanilla-colored suit, which turned out to be the bridge between the book and screen. "The introduction of Mr. Wednesday in the book and in the series had to meld," explains costume designer Suttirat Larlarb. "We couldn't diverge too

"The Vikings colonized points along a route, using giant ships that transported livestock and everything needed for the expedition to survive. Smaller, faster ships were then able to scout or ravage the next segment of the route . . . ours would have been such a ship, though a little smaller, revised for the number of Viking players. The launch was a tentative moment, but all calculations and safety checks had been made, anad we knew it was seaworthy. The day of shooting, we all watched as it came around the cape, a bit magical in the fog."
—*Patti Podesta, production designer*

much from that initial description of him in the melted vanilla ice cream suit."

Executive producer Michael Green recalls the creation of the suit as a turning point in the costume design process: "One thing that Ian said about his own wardrobes was 'Find the coat, find the man.' He had it in his head that he needed a signature coat that he could wear all the time. It would become a part of his silhouette. Suttirat built the coat, and I had the pleasure of being in the room when Ian saw it for the first time. He tried it on, looked at himself in the mirror, put his hands in his pockets, and went, 'Yeah, that's about right!'"

Larlarb says, "Ian's response to my first selection of images for him was, 'I like that you hit on the maestro about town.' That phrase always stuck with me. There was an easy, confident, bold, and powerful casualness about him. Even though we used exquisitely tailored, beautiful fabrics, together there's an eccentricity and casualness. I don't think we ever buttoned his collar, he never wore a tie, but he has a power that comes from being stately and casual."

The tiepin described in the novel was made and tried, but ultimately it and the tie were put aside—even though Wednesday's iconic tree has graced the cover of many of the book's forty-plus printings. "We made a version of it and it was beautiful," Larlarb explains, "but it weirdly did not look natural on Ian and the way he inhabited this role. It felt like a brand, like the pin was wearing him rather than him wearing the pin."

"*American Gods* is a story about faith. There's something for everybody. When you watch it, you'll have your own interpretation of it. Some people will find it sacrilegious, and other people won't find it sacrilegious enough."

—Ian McShane

"*Do you know me, Shadow?*" *said Wednesday. He rode his wolf with his head high. His right eye glittered and flashed, his left eye was dull. He wore a cloak, with a deep, monk-like cowl, and his face stared out at them from the shadows. "I told you I would tell you my names. This is what they call me. I am called Glad-of-War, Grim, Raider, and Third. I am One-Eyed. I am called Highest, and True-Guesser. I am Grimnir, and I am the Hooded One. I am All-Father, and I am Gondlir Wand-Bearer. I have as many names as there are winds, as many titles as there are ways to die. My ravens are Huginn and Muninn: Thought and Memory; my wolves are Freki and Geri; my horse is the gallows.*"

—American Gods, *chapter 6*

The Mythology of Odin

Odin is a god of many names, guises, and contradictions, as might be expected of a figure who meant many things to diverse groups of people. His worship and stories span centuries and cross much of the continent of Europe. Often depicted as a one-eyed, long-bearded man, he is the god of war and death, and he is associated with charms and magic, as well as the quest for knowledge. Odin is the All-Father of the Nordic gods, and he is often accompanied by mythical beasts, including the crows Huginn and Muninn, who bring him information from across the land.

Odin's name can be translated as Master of Ecstasy, meaning fury and passion, a sort of mad joy. This is manifest particularly in his stature as a war god. During war, Odin acts less like the traditional noble warrior and more like a leader of the berserkers. Odin seems to take joy in leading otherwise peaceful people into the chaos of battle, regardless of the reasons or justifications for the fight. On the battlefield, he gratefully receives countless human sacrifices as offerings. A warrior might also secure his favor by throwing a spear over his enemies with the call, "Odin owns ye all!"

Known as a wanderer, he at times sets out on self-interested quests, using his trickery and cunning in his never-ending pursuit of knowledge and power.

"Have a little faith.

—MR. WEDNESDAY,
EPISODE 3

LAURA MOON

🌙

"LAURA IS APPEALING BECAUSE SHE DOESN'T GIVE A SHIT. THAT'S GENERALLY SOMETHING WE FIND ATTRACTIVE IN PEOPLE."

—EMILY BROWNING

THE RANGE OF ROLES for female characters on television ha made some strides over the past decades, but women are stil often typecast into supporting roles. Meanwhile, leading ladie have to walk a fine line to be likable, interesting, and relatable while still maintaining the individuality that makes a characte and a show, tick. Emily Browning, cast as Shadow's deceitfu and soon undead wife Laura in *American Gods*, wanted to pus her role beyond that likability threshold. She sees Laura as a antihero, reprehensible and yet compelling, a type of leading lad who is rarely seen.

"So often you read about female characters who are goo girls or bad girls," Browning explained. "There's no midd ground. There have rarely been female characters who are th antihero, like Walter White, where you can't help but like hi because you've gotten to know him, but the things that he's doin are completely deplorable." The character of Laura offered th opportunity and then some. She's entitled, manipulative, sel centered, and petty. And that's all before Laura comes back fror the dead! In fact, dying is one of the best things that could hav happened to her, giving her a much-needed dose of perspective

Laura's portrayal in the book is much slimmer than in the series; she comes in and out of the story but does not drive the plot. Co-showrunners Bryan Fuller and Michael Green decided to step back in time to develop her backstory, starting from before Laura and Shadow meet. This gives audiences a fuller sense of who Laura is as well as her motivations. "When we told the tale from Laura's perspective," Fuller comments, "it felt like we could see magic from where we were standing. It was a tale that we could make our own because so much of what Laura is doing was not explored in the book."

Significant aspects of Laura's story in the book still appear on-screen—her resurrection via Sweeney's magic coin, her slow decay as the days pass, and her protection of Shadow from various perilous encounters. But in the series, Laura brings so much more to the table. She is the unfaithful lover made whole again, pursuing Shadow, life, and love with the devotion of the converted. This version of Laura was written by Fuller and Green, in consultation with Neil Gaiman, and during the first season, she evolved further based on conversations with Browning and how her performance was shaping the character.

Episode 4, "Git Gone," presents Laura's backstory, her death, her return from

"LAURA GREW UP WITHOUT TOO MANY STRUGGLES, I THINK. HER FAMILY WAS QUITE WEALTHY, AND SHE'S THE TYPE OF PERSON WHO MAY HAVE THOUGHT GREAT THINGS WERE GOING TO HAPPEN TO HER, BUT SHE NEVER MADE MUCH OF AN EFFORT."

: EMILY BROWNING :

the dead, and her reunion with Shadow in his hotel room. A new director, Craig Zobel, was brought in to helm the episode (director David Slade directed the first three episodes), and Zobel was excited by the challenge. This was the first time that the TV series would significantly expand the source material for the screen, taking viewers into uncharted territory not included in the book.

From the beginning Zobel understood that Browning did not want to play Laura as the sympathetic wife. But he also knew that audiences needed to relate to her. Much like the character Walter White in the series *Breaking Bad*—who reveals he has cancer in the first episode—Laura is revealed to suffer from a profound dissatisfaction, bordering on suicidal depression. "We needed to show an inner struggle so that the audience would have sympathy," Zobel elaborates. "Even if outwardly she makes a lot of terrible choices."

Though executive producers Fuller and Green along with David Slade had already established a visual tone for the series, they wanted Zobel to take episode 4 in a new direction. "For Laura's episode," Zobel explains, "because it wasn't beholden to fans' expectations of the story line, I felt I could come at it a bit differently. Bryan

encouraged me to watch *Lost in Translation*, which seemed like an unusual reference. But as I talked to him more, I grasped what he was looking for. It's a very interpersonal story."

Though he handed over the reins after the first three episodes, Slade laid the foundation for Laura's physical appearance, as well as the particular way she sees the world post-mortem. Being dead, he reasoned, would not only affect her looks. It would also change her vision. After much thought and research, Slade came up with what he refers to as "Laura vision." "If you see from the point of view of the dead," Slade explains, "You can't see the way we're seeing. Your organs are all dead. So we brought in more of the visual infrared light spectrum."

DEATH BECOMES HER

LAURA'S CHARACTER ARC is full of dramatic irony: Only once she's dead does she finally find a purpose and something worth living for. She loves Shadow and pursues him and Mr. Wednesday across America, becoming Shadow's guardian angel along the way. "When she's alive, Laura can't really feel love," Browning comments. "She doesn't know what it is. After she dies, Shadow becomes her god. Honestly, if that had been the initial pitch of the character, I don't think I would have been

interested. She worships her husband?! Sounds kind of awful. But that's not who she is. Her god becomes love, which causes her to do this 180."

One problem, of course, is that while she finds Shadow infinitely more attractive, she herself loses a considerable amount of sex appeal. Decomposing, sewn-together, and for a time, holding her severed arm, she fits no one's definition of attractive. But, proving the old adage that beauty is only skin deep, Laura reveals an incredible amount of charm and power in her undead state.

One of the things that makes Laura compelling, dead or alive, is the fact that she truly does not care what anyone else thinks of her. This is a helpful state of mind when you smell like a meat locker on a sunny day and have a constant entourage of flies. "Laura's my favorite character," Ricky Whittle comments. "She's broken and damaged, but she's honest about the things that she does. She's very adamant about having Shadow back, despite her horrific scarring and that she's not even alive! It's a very interesting dynamic."

LAURA AND SHADOW

IN ANOTHER IRONY, Mr. Wednesday causes Laura to be killed in a car accident so she won't get in the way of his

"A lot of what we do is propelled by this knowledge that one day we're going to die. For Laura, that keeps her in a frustrated place because she doesn't know what to do. So when she dies, she's like, 'Oh, I'm still here,' and it makes her a better person because she has no fear. It doesn't necessarily make her a kinder person, but she realizes that Shadow is the person that she wants to be with. She becomes his slightly evil guardian angel."
—Emily Browning

plans for Shadow after he is released from prison. But alive, the couple was probably doomed. Only once Laura returns undead do she and Shadow seem capable of building a better and more honest relationship. Apparently, having your cheating wife come back from the dead restarts the conversation.

And they have some real issues to work through. Laura didn't want Shadow when she was alive, at least not the kind, BBQ'ing, hardworking Shadow that he became. She wanted the criminal, risk-taking Shadow she glimpsed when they first met. "Laura was attracted to Shadow because he seemed dangerous to her," Browning explains. "It's like she was smacking her head against the wall to try and feel something. Then he turns out to be lovely and sweet and he wants the classic American family. She wanted to be with someone who made her feel alive, ironically enough."

In fact, Shadow is so lovestruck with Laura at the beginning of the series that, for his part, Whittle had a hard time connecting with him. "I remember Ricky feeling that Shadow was kind of pathetic," Browning recalls. "He would say, 'I hate him! Why does he love her so much when she's so awful to him?' We talked about it, and I explained how to me it makes him more of a hero. That's a very strong word, but he knows that she has issues, and he still believes that one day she's going to be okay. He takes care of her, he sees her pain, and he loves her. If anything, that frustrates her more. She wants a fight."

Once Laura comes back from the dead, she is more than ready to move on from her past betrayals, but Shadow still has plenty of questions, anger, and distrust to work through. It's a classic romantic dramedy with a fantastical twist.

FIGHTING THE CHILDREN

LAURA COMES BACK from the dead just in time. In episode 4, we see her return to find Shadow dangling from a tree in the middle of a barren, rain-soaked field, surrounded by a gang of the Children, Technical Boy's faceless minions, there to do his brutal bidding. It's the same scene that ends episode 1, when it is presented from Shadow's point of view. In this way, the lynching becomes a bridge between Shadow's and Laura's points of view, and their alternating story lines progress through the rest of season 1.

Episode 4 director Craig Zobel found that filming this scene posed a unique challenge. By then, several months had passed since director David Slade had filmed episode 1. Now Zobel had to re-create that set and shoot a complex fight scene in the middle of a manufactured downpour; but nothing looked the same. Since Slade's shoot, spring had come and gone. The once-barren field was now awash in waist-high rows of corn, and in the middle, the winter-bare tree was fully leafed and green.

How to contact us

Main switchboard 812-555-4401
Placing an ad? 812-555-4310
Placing a classified? 812-555-2183
Placing an obituary? 812-555-4339
Subscriber services 812-555-4200
Talk to the editor? 812-555-4364
Did you find a mistake? .. 812-555-1460

MISSED YOUR PAPER? If you are unable to contact your newspaper carrier, or have service questions, call 812-555-4200 or 800-555-0070.
SEE AN ERROR? If you see an error in The Herald-Times, let us know by calling 812-555-1460 or by sending an email to mistakes@heraldt.com.net

Serving Monroe, Bartholomew, Brown, Greene, Lawrence, Marion, Martin, Morgan, Orange and Owen counties.

Founded in 1877 as the Telephone; Evening World founded in 1892; World and Telephone consolidated in 1943; Herald established in 1947; Herald-Telephone consolidated in 1950; Herald-Times renamed in 1989.

Member of: Inland Daily Press Assn., sier State Press Assn., Associated Newspaper Association of Americ
The Herald-Times (ISSN 794-7936) published daily except on Sundays. Christmas by the Herald-Times, Inc. S. Walnut St., Bloomington, IN 474 is also a participant in the Hoosier newspaper published on Sundays.

HT HeraldTimesOnline.com is free to seven-day office-pay subscribers to The Herald-Times or $8.95 a month for others. See HeraldTimesOnline.com/su

OBITUARIES

Laura Moon, 27
OCT. 23, 1990 – APRIL 14, 2017

EAGLE POINT – Laura Moon, age 27, of Eagle Point, Indiana, was killed in the early hours Wednesday morning in an automobile accident. Laura loved her work, her friends and her family. She is survived by her husband, Shadow; her mother, Marilyn; her sister and family, and her paternal grandparents, Buck and Betty McCabe. A dealer at the 26th Dynasty Casino, Laura enjoyed spending time with her family, her friends, and with her cat Dummy. Her family, friends, and community, will mourn her loss greatly. All are invited to attend Laura's memorial service at Saint Monica's Church.

grandmother, Anna Mitchell, grandfather, Russell Mitchell, and grandfather, Nobel Connor. Rickey will be remembered as a talented musician.

Please come share your memories 6 to 8 p.m. Friday, March 11, 2016, at The Funeral Chapel of Powell and Deckard, 3000 E. Third St., Bloomington, IN 47401. Memories of Rickey and condolences may be made to the family at www.the funeralchapel.net.

Gordon Robert Peterson, 78
NOV. 25, 1938 – MARCH 7, 2017

BLOOMINGTON — Frederick Russell Ogan died on Monday, March 7, 2016, after his battle with cancer. Fred was born Nov. 25, 1938, in Gary, Indiana, to the late Russell and Veronica Ogan.

He was married 54 years to Carol (Lahaie) Ogan. Children include son, Lt. Scott F. Ogan, wife Michelle (Donahue) Ogan, daughter, Sherilyn M. (Ogan) Fosha, husband, Joel Fosha, son, Rodney A. Ogan, wife, Lori G. (Ogan) Ogan. Grandchildren include Katie Ogan, Nathan Ogan, Veronica

Gordon

McLoughlin

Sean Edward McLoughlin, 86
SEPT. 12, 1930 – MARCH 7, 2017

NASHVILLE — Wayne Carter Brahaum, age 85, of Nashville, Indiana, died Monday morning at his residence. Born Sept. 12, 1930, in Indianapolis, Indiana, he was the son of Vora Mae (Reese) Brahaum and Albert C. Brahaum. He temporarily served in the U.S. Army until it was determined he was just 15 years of age. Also in his younger years he was employed as a concrete truck driver, then a chauffeur at the Job Corps at Camp Atterbury. In 1968 he switched careers and became a deputy sheriff with the Brown County Sheriff's Department until retiring in 1992. After retirement he worked as a security officer, first at the Monroe County Justice Building in Bloomington and later at the Bloomington Hospital until finally retiring in 2010. He is survived by his wife, Shirley (Mask) Brahaum

will be 10-11 a.m. Saturday at First Church of the Nazarene in Spencer. Services will be 11 a.m. Saturday at the church. West & Parrish & Pedigo Funeral Home in Spencer is in charge of arrangements.

Katy Thatcher, 90
JUNE 19, 1926 – MARCH 1, 2017

WHITTIER, N.C. — Wilma Abram, a long-time resident of Bloomington, IN, passed away at Mission-St. Joseph Hospital in Asheville, NC, March 1, 2016.

She was born June 19, 1926, to Frank Bryant and May Pedro Bryant and was preceded in death by her husband, Robert William Abram, and brothers, Frank Bryant, Jr. and Dennis Bryant.

Katy

She is survived by her son, Robert Michael Abram, M.D., and his wife, Susan, and sister, Esther Bryant Arnold. Grandchildren include grandson Wade Abram and spouse Desiree, and Christa Williamson and spouse Dwight. Wilma had seven great-grandchildren: Alyssa, Andrew, Emma and Carson Abram, and Cole Saunooke and Reese and Elle Williamson. She had

Polic dies heroi
By Sonia C
812-555-4245 | at

Bloomin a 25-year-
after possib in his best fr day evening
Investi called to M for a repor overdose p p.m. Sunday
Logan Spencer, ha hospital by arrived.
His frien the two ha ing out in and went t the east sid friend said l

POL
By Valerie
812-555-4245 | at

THEFT
■ 600 block Avenue, 5:27 employees at reported four an outdoor ta food and drin

EYE OF HORUS

ASP

COBRA HEADS

26th DYNASTY CASINO DEALER UNIFORM
AMERICAN GODS EP 105

OPTION 1:
PYRAMID BROCADE.
+
ASP BOWTIE

So the production crew set to work clearing a large area of corn and pulling leaves from the part of the tree that would be in frame. "Some part of me felt so guilty, poor tree," Zobel admits. "I hope it was okay at the end of the day."

In addition, Zobel needed to figure out how to coordinate Laura's trajectory through the scene in such a way that it fit within the original blocking, but revealed a new point of view. He and the crew spent a lot of time prepping the shoot, storyboarding, and blocking out the action. The shoot required that multiple departments come together for planning and execution. For example, the scene in which Laura kicks the spine out of one of the Children started with the stunts, wardrobe, special-effects, camera, and makeup effects teams all huddled around the storyboards, weighing in on how the story beat would be best accomplished. Once they agreed upon the basic approach, the teams got to work. Stunts blocked the action in a rehearsal, practical effects and makeup built and tested the rigs that provide the blood spray and separate the dummy from the physical skeleton, and wardrobe figured out a version of the costume to facilitate the split. Then visual effects stepped in to advise on how these disparate parts could come together with a bit of CG stitching. "In a perfect world," explains VFX supervisor Jeremy Ball, "all of these practical efforts, combined with some strategic camera placement, would mean that additional visual effects work wouldn't be needed at all. The footage that's shot on the day can go straight into the show. In reality, what happens is that some things go according to plan (great kick!), some things don't (wasn't the blood supposed to be a geyser?), and something magical happens that no one expected (did you see what they caught on C camera?). In the end, for this scene, we added some blood to a couple of the shots and provided the skeleton, which needed to be entirely computer generated."

Zobel and the cast and crew shot over two nights. First Laura sees Shadow hanging in the tree. Then she starts to fight, and the action speeds up as Laura pivots from one adversary to the next. In reality, filming this frenetic battle slowed to a painful crawl, as water from the rain machines turned the recently plowed field into a giant mud bath.

"Poor Emily," Zobel recalls. "There were times where she was literally up to her knees in mud. Everything was in slow motion—it took so much longer than I had anticipated."

WHAT DO YOU WEAR WHEN YOU'RE DEAD?

COMPARED TO THE gods, Laura's wardrobe is very limited, and once she's undead, clothing for her is purely functional. Zombies aren't exactly fashion-conscious. Still, a lot of thought went into Laura's clothing.

Costume designer Suttirat Larlarb considered wear and tear when designing Laura's undead outfit. Would it get rained on? Be covered in blood? Ripped? Shredded? How far could they

push the material before it would become unusable? Then there is her right arm, which comes off and is later sewn back on. In episode 4, Laura returns to her friend Audrey's house to borrow some craft supplies to stitch herself back together, and this scene inspired an unfortunate choice of top. "When we were doing the tests," Browning recalls, "I had the stitches on my shoulder. So we thought, 'Oh, we'll put a tank top on because it's really cool that you can see the scar on her shoulder.' We quickly regretted that decision because it meant that I had to get that shoulder makeup put on every day, which was an hour-and-a-half-long process."

Even when the arm was detached, it required some filmmaking magic to achieve the desired effect on-screen. Browning was fitted with a blue sleeve that extended from the tips of her fingers up to her shoulder joint, which enabled the VFX team to remove it from the shot in post-production. The only problem was that when they removed the arm, they were left with a blank space in its place, which they needed to re-create. This wasn't too big of a deal when they had

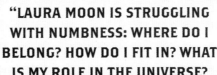

"LAURA MOON IS STRUGGLING WITH NUMBNESS: WHERE DO I BELONG? HOW DO I FIT IN? WHAT IS MY ROLE IN THE UNIVERSE? WHAT IS THIS LIFE THAT I AM LIVING, AND WHAT'S THE POINT? RIGHT UP UNTIL THE MOMENT SHE LOSES IT."

: BRYAN FULLER :
EXECUTIVE PRODUCER

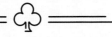

to fill in the background of a scene, but if the arm crossed over Browning's body at all during a shoot, the fix process was considerably more complicated. "If Emily's blue arm is between herself and the camera," explains Jeremy Ball, VFX supervisor, "and you remove the arm, you now need to re-create the parts of the actress that were once hidden by it: her wardrobe, her torso, and potentially even her face and hair. All of this is possible. It just takes time and money with arguably very little payoff on the screen. If you watch the episode you'll notice that whenever possible we've minimized opportunities for Laura to be 'upstaged' by her arm. Of course, there are moments where this can't be avoided, like when Laura is packing her bag after taking a shower and the scene necessitated a big camera move around her. There's really no staging solution, so you just bite the bullet and commit."

In episode 7, they finally solved that problem. Previously, Larlarb had found a vintage 1960s red baseball jacket on one of her shopping trawls of Toronto. She had it in mind for Laura, but she had not found the right moment in the show to use it.

It didn't seem like something that Laura would own, and it was too iconic for a backstory garment. Then, as they prepared for the ice cream truck scene in episode 7, Larlarb had an inspiration. "I thought to myself, 'Oh, what if it's the ice cream truck driver's jacket?'" Larlarb recalls. "And when she gets in the accident, she can use it to hold herself together?" In the accident, Laura splits open the stitches on her torso; and afterward, she doesn't take the jacket off for the rest of the season. As Larlarb predicted, it fits her fearless undead persona perfectly.

ZOMBIE EFFECTS

EMILY BROWNING WILL admit it wasn't much of a stretch for her to achieve the pallor of death. Already pale, she lost what little color she had after a few weeks of all-day and late-night shoots. By the season's final episodes, she had acquired some authentic under-eye shadows, and she recalls that the makeup artists could create her undead complexion with just a half hour in the chair. Colin Penman, head of makeup, doesn't go quite as far in his recollection of her pallor. "Though I don't think she would use the color I put on her as a foundation in real life," he comments, "she's certainly not a child of the sun. But I wouldn't go as far as she did, that she looked like a cadaver."

Browning found being undead freeing. Rather than keeping her hair perfect and her look polished, she could let it all go. "When we were doing camera tests at the beginning," Browning recalls, "I asked Bryan and Michael, 'What do you want to do with my hair?' And they said, 'Nothing. Maybe make it a bit more wavy and messy.' Then I asked, 'What about my armpits? Do I have to shave them?' And they said, 'No, leave them like that.' It was great! There's only so much you can do when your body starts to rot."

The prosthetics, on the other hand, were complex and time-consuming. The Y incision Shadow sees when Laura gets out of the bath in his hotel room took four hours to apply. And the scenes where Laura carries her detached arm were a challenge. Wielding the prosthetic arm was fun, but Browning had to act with her real arm held away from her body, encased in a blue sleeve up to the shoulder so that the visual effects crew could edit it out in post-production. "When we were shooting the scene at Audrey's house," Browning recalls, "I opened the door to the bathroom, and after the first take they said, 'That was great! But let's do it again. You opened the door with your arm that doesn't exist.'"

However, the most intricate prosthetic built for Laura was her throat. In episode 5, Mad Sweeney looks down her gullet and sees his magic coin. Rather than use visual effects to film the sequence, the physical effects team, headed by Christien Tinsley, built a model of Laura's esophagus and guts, into which they sent the camera. As Tinsley recalls: "We see the camera

do this move into the interior of her mouth, down the back of her throat, into the cavernous abyss of her belly, where we see the gold coin resting in the side of her belly cavity. That was all done practically using actual model materials, rather than VFX. Imagine a mouth on the end of a long snake tube, and we drew the camera down into this diorama of a belly. Those kinds of effects are extremely challenging, and in some ways, I think nowadays would often be left to visual effects."

AUDREY AND ROBBIE

TWO UNEXPECTED STARS of the first season are Audrey and Robbie, Laura and Shadow's friends, played by Betty Gilpin and Dane Cook, respectively. Though they have a limited number of scenes, they are memorable, pivotal characters in the story.

Betty Gilpin surprised the showrunners with her take on Laura's best friend. In episode 4, when she sees Laura in her house for the first time after the funeral, she manages to be tragic, terrified, and helpful, practically within the same breath. The showrunners knew that the relationship between Laura and Audrey had potential, but Gilpin showed them how entertaining it could be. "Betty Gilpin walked such a tightrope in her performance," Fuller recalls. "It was masterful in its alchemy, weaving between funny,

raw, and vulnerable emotions. Every time I see the scene of her at the graveyard it makes me cry because, even though she is buzzed out of her head on Ativan, she is a human being having a very complicated experience and being an utterly charming mess about the whole thing."

Gilpin's comedic skills brought out the funny in other characters as well. When director Craig Zobel worked with Gilpin on episode 4, he realized that there was a lot of humor within the show's dramatic fantasy. "Betty really brought it to the table," Zobel recalls. "For both me and Emily, after working with her, we were like, 'Oh, now I know how to do this. We can be funny and serious.' Betty is instinctively a very, very funny person."

As for stand-up comic Dane Cook, his comedic reputation precedes him, and the showrunners were excited to fold his specific brand of humor into *American Gods*. He was the perfect person to portray Robbie, a relatively simple and simple-minded man who is obligated to service his desires, both big-headed and littleheaded, and can't help getting himself into trouble. Despite Laura's clear parameters on their affair, Robbie still falls for her. Unfortunately, his untimely demise in the car crash with Laura would seem to signal the end of his story line in *American Gods*. That is, short of someone tossing another magic coin into Robbie's grave.

"Physics doesn't take Sundays off."

—LAURA MOON

Mad Sweeney

Episode 7's "Coming to America" interlude tells the story of Essie Tregowan, the Irishwoman responsible for bringing Mad Sweeney to America in the eighteenth century. Essie is played by Emily Browning, the same actress cast as Laura, Shadow's dead wife. This double casting came about after Fuller and Green spent some time searching for a leading lady for the vignette. They were not having much luck when they hit upon the idea of casting Browning in the role. It deviated from the telling in the book, where there is no connection, implied or explicit, between Essie and Laura. But the suggestion that this casting weaves on the screen, though never stated directly within the script, strengthens some of the other changes they made to the story. "In the final analysis, when you watch the episode, you get the haunting feeling that perhaps Laura is a reincarnation of Essie," explains Adam Kane, the episode's director and an executive producer. "That was not the original intention for the scene—but connecting Laura and Essie's stories ended up adding dimension to the overall story arc, which in turn makes Mad Sweeney's journey more human. Up until that point, we only get one dimension of him: He's this ornery, mischievous character. In Essie's story and episode 7 you realize that he has spent centuries suffering for the sake of this one woman, and that he's given up some of his own life in order for Laura and Shadow's lives to evolve."

The double casting was a challenge worthy of Browning, who was more than happy to trade her bloodied tank top for a wardrobe of eighteenth-century frocks. "Browning is incredible," Kane comments. "Embracing and embodying two distinctly different but echoing characters—Essie and Laura—is no small task. She brought a superb, deft touch in her approach to each character. Making distinctive choices about her performance was a big part of what we worked on together, making sure that Essie is guarded enough when she first meets Mad Sweeney in the prison, but that her adventurous spirit is also open enough to allow him in. That's not something that Laura Moon would do if she met Mad Sweeney in the present."

The story of Essie and Mad Sweeney explores both the mythology of leprechauns and the way a lady of little means might gain independence and power in Georgian England—namely, by stealing. As long as she pays her dues with a bit of bread or coin, Essie seems to share the luck of her guardian leprechaun, Mad Sweeney. With his help, she escapes jail and a death sentence before finally becoming an indentured servant on a tobacco farm in Virginia. In the end, her leprechaun returns for her, taking her hand as she dies an old woman peeling apples on the porch. She is one of his last true believers, a woman of the old country who paid her dues to the fair folk until her last days.

This "Coming to America" story was a dream for the costume and production design teams. On the production side it was a massive undertaking, more akin to a mini-movie than a television show. The story spans nearly eighty years of history—we see Essie from when she was a young girl in Ireland to when she is an older woman in Colonial America. Browning had twenty-nine costume changes for Essie alone and the set design crew created Oxford Street, London, in the eighteenth century, as well as a Virginia tobacco farm and frontier house, with lots of help from VFX. "Neil Gaiman is very particular about historical accuracy," Kane explains, "so we spent a lot of time researching details. In the Oxford market, for example, we found out what they would have sold, how the market would have been set up, what one would have been arrested and tried for, and what the penalty would have been."

Costume designer Suttirat Larlarb was once a professor of costume history, and she flexed her costume-crafting skills in a way seldom available outside of feature films. Essie journeys from the kitchen of a rural Irish estate to the bustling streets of London, to a ship full of indentured servants, and finally to Colonial America. Larlarb and her team designed every stitch of her costumes, which was necessary both to achieve the desired level of detail and authenticity and to fit Browning's diminutive frame. "It was such a gift to be able to do a survey of a century of women's clothing on one character," Larlarb recalls. "The hats, the ribbons, the hooks and eyes, even every bit of the trimming on the corset and layers of petticoats, were made from scratch."

Another thing made from scratch is the piles of food on display in the Oxford Street market where Essie wanders in search of an easy wallet or trinket to steal. It might seem like it would have been easier to use props for most of it, given that it is part of the setting, but food stylist Janice Poon has learned the hard way not to take such shortcuts. "The food is all real because you never know—a director might come on to a set and say, 'Oh, yeah! Just stand over there and grab a little hand pie and take a bite out of it.' It's not in the script, but you have to be ready. As a food stylist, if I'm bringing anything to the set that looks edible, it has to be edible."

"Malice draped in pretty can get away with murder."

—Mr. Ibis, episode 7

MAD SWEENEY

> "I WAS A KING ONCE. THEN THEY MADE ME A BIRD. THEN MOTHER CHURCH CAME AND TURNED ALL OF US INTO FAIRIES AND TROLLS AND SAINTS, AND GENERAL MILLS DID THE REST." —MAD SWEENEY, EPISODE 8

MAD SWEENEY IS THE itinerant lanky leprechaun who does Mr. Wednesday's bidding, but like Wednesday, Sweeney is a much-diminished god. "Mad Sweeney is a leprechaun who has lost his luck," explains Pablo Schreiber, the actor who plays Sweeney. "He was brought over by some believers in the 1700s from Ireland. He ended up bouncing around and losing influence, losing followers, and like many of the Old Gods in our story, is down on his luck."

Casting the part experienced its own run of bad luck at first. Sean Harris was originally cast to play Sweeney, but he had to drop out early in filming due to personal reasons. One man's ill luck is another's fortune, however, and Schreiber (well-known from *The Wire* and *Orange Is the New Black*) stepped into Mad Sweeney's oversized eighteenth-century boots. He had a window of time in his schedule in which the *American Gods* production fit perfectly.

All still wasn't smooth sailing. Harris had already completed a week of shooting and made certain choices about the character's portrayal that didn't fit Schreiber and how he wanted to embody this mythological legend. At the same time, due to production design issues, the production crew had to reshoot several scenes, including the epic brawl in the Crocodile Bar. Ultimately the reshoot provided an opportunity to accommodate Schreiber and the tweaks in his portrayal, which set the final tone for the Mad Sweeney we know today.

Ultimately, Schreiber is a perfect fit for Mad Sweeney. He captures the god's punchy Irish wit and uses the full force of his six-foot-five frame to push Sweeney's physicality and prankster menace to the edge of reason. In episode 1, when Sweeney challenges Shadow to a fight in the Crocodile Bar, it's clear that he takes real pleasure in the fight. It's not just a job he needs to do for Mr. Wednesday—for a leprechaun, it's the ideal way to pass the time.

CRACKING A WINDOW ON THE WORLD

MAD SWEENEY'S STORY in the TV series has been expanded tremendously from the book, where he appears only briefly in the first few chapters. "Mad Sweeney's only in two scenes in the book," Schreiber recalls. "There's tons of time in between in which you don't know where he's at. And this is what the TV show fills in. That's the joy of it, creating something separate from the novel that still exists in the world of it."

Most of all, in the book, the undead Laura and Mad Sweeney never cross paths, and Sweeney ends up frozen to death in an alley, having lost his gold coin and completely run out of luck. Yet the TV series gives Sweeney a new lease on life. We get to watch as Mad Sweeney careens after Laura, whose return from the dead is thanks to her possession of his magic coin, until he eventually joins in her madcap pursuit of Shadow, thus uniting these two characters in one of television's oddest road-tripping adventures.

In season 2, the *American Gods* story lines and characters will likely continue to diverge from the book in all sorts of small, significant, and unexpected ways, but that's the fun of it. "We want to show the world just what a wonderful book it is and what we particularly love about it," executive producer Michael Green explains. "There are moments we looked at in the novel where we knew we needed to be faithful. Then there are places

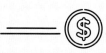

"I NEVER EXPECTED TO FALL IN LOVE WITH MAD SWEENEY. PABLO'S PERFORMANCE IS ASTONISHING BECAUSE, YES, HE'S SAYING THE SAME LINES THAT SWEENEY SAID IN THE BOOK, BUT THERE'S SO MUCH CHARM IN THEM. HE'S WONDERFUL."

: NEIL GAIMAN :

where we felt that we had acres of room for expansion. We saw the book as a window cracked open to an entire world."

FINDING LAURA

THE EXPANSION FROM book to screen of Mad Sweeney and his relationship with Laura touched many scenes. From his confrontation with Laura in a hotel room to hijacking an ice cream truck and, in the season's final episode, winding up at Easter's mansion with the whole motley crew, the on-screen Sweeney is a far cry from the desperate, alcoholic leprechaun of the book. This Sweeney is passionate and complex, bereft but pragmatic, and perhaps a little smitten.

"The relationship between Laura and Sweeney is so much fun," exclaims actress Emily Browning, who plays Laura. "He's a big, towering dude and I'm five-foot-one. But Laura has this superhuman strength after she dies, so there is always this undercurrent of 'I could beat the shit out of you if I wanted to.' It made the dynamic really interesting."

Laura's physical and emotional strength seems to charm Mad Sweeney. Though Laura may be a zombie and beginning to fall apart at the seams, Sweeney can't help but fall under her spell. She's as much a force of nature as he is, and she doesn't back down when faced with his bluster and guff. Further, the season's final episode reveals a twist that helps explain Sweeney's feelings. We return to an earlier scene and again witness Laura's car careening out of control, leaving her dead body in a twisted heap, but our perspective is revealed to be from Sweeney's eyes. He looks over the result of his handiwork, in the service of Mr. Wednesday, and this murder shapes Sweeney's relationship to Laura from the moment of their post-death confrontation in Shadow's motel room.

"Sweeney finds Laura fascinating," Schreiber explains. "He falls in love with her a bit while he's watching her at Mr. Wednesday's behest, though then he's forced to kill her. He has all this guilt about it—at bottom he's not a bad person. He just does things for Mr. Wednesday because he always has."

A THROWBACK STYLE

FROM HEAD TO toe, Sweeney's style is an amalgam of the times he has passed through. More than the other gods, who tend to have an iconic, unchanging look, Sweeney is a fly strip for fashion, collecting bits and pieces of the hipster trends of the twentieth

"Sweeney and Laura are on the road together because they have to be. They each need something from the other, but they really can't stand each other. Being able to have those scenes together, to rip into each other the whole time, was something I hadn't been able to do before. It was really fun."

—Emily Browning

"For one reason or another, Sweeney is desperately indebted to Mr. Wednesday. He's been an enforcer for Wednesday for at least the last fifty to sixty years. Doing anything that would upset him in Wednesday's eyes is not an option."

—Pablo Schreiber

leprechauny elements. "His look started with the jacket," Larlarb elaborates. "It isn't a traditional jean trucker jacket. It's almost like a denim Norfolk country sporting jacket, which has a belt and multiple pockets. It has an Old World, nineteenth-century quality to it mixed with the seventies, but updated by denim. His pants are based on a pair of vintage trousers, which could fit into his tall eighteenth-century boots if needed. In fact, the boots that he wears as Mad Sweeney in the Essie Tregowan *Coming to America* scenes are the same boots he wears as contemporary Mad Sweeney."

Beyond the vintage American fashion, Sweeney's costume hides touches of the mythological, if you know where to look. While leprechauns of Irish legend were more prone to dwell in forests than dive bars, Sweeney carries their mischief and luck, and a bit of their look, forward into the twenty-first century. The birds on the patch on his jacket relate to his bird state in the tale of Buile Suibhne, his origin fable in Irish mythology, in which he nests in a yew tree.

Sweeney's recasting posed a challenge for the costume department, which had to make adjustments midshoot. For one thing, at six-foot-five, Schreiber is larger than Harris, but more than that, Harris's take on Sweeney was more rockabilly and Western and more aggressive. Harris's Sweeney had snakeskin boots and a vintage suede Western jacket, and the colors in his costume complemented the actor's coloring as a natural redhead. Further, the wig they had originally developed for Harris didn't work with Schreiber's frame and complexion.

"The wig didn't look very good on me," Schreiber recalls. "They had modeled it off a picture of Tom Waits from the late sixties or seventies, which was perfect for the character. But when they put it on my head, it looked messy. I had just finished shooting a movie where I played a white supremacist skinhead, so my head was all shaved. I said, 'What if we cut out the sides and make it a faux-hawk?' It worked! It was terrifying to take scissors to the wig, but as soon as the sides came out, the whole thing just looked more authentic on my head." Karola Dirnberger, the lead hair designer, has a similar recollection of the wig-fitting process: "I spent much of a long weekend at Pablo's hotel working on the wig. Because it's a wig, you want to be careful. You can't just put things back onto it, it doesn't grow back. So how far could we cut it? It was a great experience, because the more we cut, the more he was starting to feel like Mad Sweeney. Watching him become the character as we were creating that piece on the head, it was just the most amazing thing."

century. "We wanted his costume to be a mishmash of stuff that he's gathered throughout the decades," Schreiber explains. "The jacket looks like it's from the late fifties, early sixties. The boots could easily be from the forties or fifties. The shirt is kind of a modern cowboy shirt." The resulting look wouldn't be out of place in the trendy throwback culture of LA's Silver Lake or Brooklyn's Williamsburg neighborhoods, though Sweeney comes with a touch more authenticity, having lived through the eras he is wearing.

Costume designer Suttirat Larlarb took Sweeney's physicality into consideration in developing his costume. He's a rogue mischief-maker, so his costume couldn't constrict him. It needed to be movable and bar-brawly, with a little bit of protection and

According to Mr. Ibis, Mad Sweeney had started his life as the guardian of a sacred rock in a small Irish glade, over three thousand years ago. Mr. Ibis told them of Mad Sweeney's love affairs, his enmities, the madness that gave him his power . . . the worship and adoration in his own land that slowly transmuted into a guarded respect and then, finally, into amusement.

—American Gods, *chapter 8*

✥ The MYTHOLOGY of LEPRECHAUNS ✥

Mad Sweeney is no Lucky Charms leprechaun. Modern depictions of leprechauns are largely based on derogatory nineteenth-century caricatures and stereotypes of the Irish and have little relation to Irish mythology. As Mad Sweeney says in chapter 2 of *American Gods*: "You have to learn to think outside the box. . . . There's a lot more to Ireland than Guinness."

Tall and lanky, with a poet's turn of phrase and a trickster's knack for coins and bets, Sweeney is a mad and exiled king who comes over from the old country in the beliefs of Essie Tregowan, a girl from Bantry who flees a death sentence for stealing and dreams of luck and fortune in the New World. "I didn't spend too much time worrying about the bastardization of leprechauns in American culture," explains Schreiber,

"because you get that for free. We grew up with Lucky Charms and the idea of the leprechaun at the end of the rainbow. I did look into the story about the king who went crazy and spent hundreds of years flying around as a bird. The idea of bouncing around in a world that's not yours makes sense in the original mythological story, as well as in Neil's novel."

Mad Sweeney traces his origins to the twelfth century and the tale of Buile Suibhne, a provincial king driven insane by the curse of St. Ronan, who Suibhne abuses during a disagreement. St. Ronan curses Suibhne to wander the land naked, at times leaping about as a crazed bird, until he is slain by the jealous husband of a cook at a monastery where he takes lodging. ☘

"GIVE ME MY FUCKIN' COIN BACK."

— MAD SWEENEY,

EPISODE 5

THE COINS

'The power that we give objects runs through the tale of American Gods. An object is only as powerful as the faith you put into it."

—Bryan Fuller, executive producer

COINS MAKE APPEARANCES THROUGHOUT *American Gods,* driving the plot in ways large and small. From the quarters that Shadow spins across his knuckles to the shower of gold that Mad Sweeney pulls from the air, coins wield power, though this varies depending on who has them and what that person believes. In an act of disregard, Shadow casts Mad Sweeney's magic coin into Laura's grave, which expresses his deep lack of faith and inability to value what others might believe. The consequences of this follow Shadow, quite literally, as he struggles through his own evolution of faith. "The coins become a metaphor for Shadow being a nonbeliever growing to be a believer," executive producer Bryan Fuller explains. "Initially he took the thing that everybody valued and played tricks with it. He did not value it other than as a deception. Then he's given a coin that's very powerful, and he throws it away."

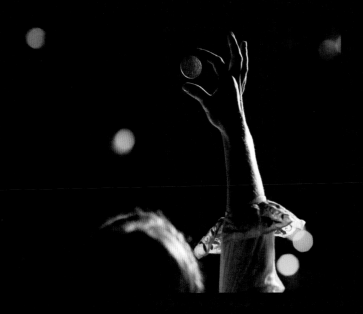

MAD SWEENEY'S ILL LUCK

UNFORTUNATELY, WHEN SWEENEY gives his magic coin away to Shadow, he gives away his luck, which is all but a death sentence for a leprechaun. The dangerous consequences of this careless act are revealed in episode 3: Sweeney hitches a ride with a kind, proselytizing, recovering alcoholic (played by Scott Thompson), but then the driver is impaled in a freak road accident. After the accident, a tow truck driver remarks, "That's some crazy bad luck," and these words strike fear into Sweeney's heart and capture the magnitude of his loss. As Schreiber explains: "Mad Sweeney can conjure gold at any moment, but he doesn't have the one coin that has given him his magic, his luck."

To recover his coin, Sweeney pursues and eventually finds Laura, but he discovers it's not so simple to get a magic coin back from an undead woman once she has it inside her chest. In the book, Laura keeps the coin in her pocket, but in the show, Laura holds it viscerally inside herself, and the coin lights and animates her from within. "The magical coin from Mad Sweeney is not like any other coin," executive producer Bryan Fuller elaborates. "Yes, it has value, but this coin can bring someone back to life. And how can Mad Sweeney take his coin back from Laura when it's keeping her alive?"

THE MOON COIN

ONE OF THE sweetest, and least fraught, moments in *American Gods* comes in episode 3, when Zorya Polunochnaya pulls the moon from the sky and hands it to Shadow in the form of a silver dollar. Shadow is nearly suicidal at this point in the story, but Polunochnaya sees potential in Shadow, a glimmer of the man he will become. "Zorya gives Shadow a coin of protection," Fuller explains. "She tells him, 'This is not the first time that you've been given a protection for your life, for the thing that you're supposed to value and that you keep throwing away. Hold on to this one, find value in this. Start to believe in it and embrace your destiny.'"

In some ways, these magic coins are more powerful than the gods, since they are beyond their control. Wednesday certainly did not plan for Laura to come back to life with one embedded where her heart should beat. More than any other character, Laura poses a threat to Wednesday's plans for Shadow and the coming war. As she comes to realize how Wednesday has manipulated her life, and as Sweeney is brought to heel by losing his coin to her, she gains the upper hand on even the gods.

JACK'S CROCODILE BAR

"American Gods *exists between two worlds.
It isn't quite fantasy, and it certainly isn't reality.
A lot of people have an idea of what magic might
look like in this world. Until we show them those
moments on their feet, like in Jack's Crocodile
Bar, they can't fully understand our adaptation."*
—Michael Green, executive producer

IN EPISODE 1, WHEN SHADOW steps into Jack's Crocodile Bar looking for a bite to eat, he has no idea that he has crossed over from the human world. This bar, it turns out, is one of only a few places that act as a bridge between the human and god realms, serving both and tolerating the attendant idiosyncrasies. Humans in the bar might be unaware of the divinity of their barmates, but they understand that unusual occurrences should be taken in stride. The gods descend soon after Shadow arrives. First, Mr. Wednesday appears at the urinal next to him, and then Mad Sweeney approaches, looking for a fight. "The Croc Bar is the first moment where we establish what 'reality' in *American Gods* will look like," explains executive producer Michael Green. "It's a bar, but it's strange. There are people, there's a beer tap, they serve food. And yet it's also a place where you might have a run-in with a seven-foot-tall leprechaun."

lights and crocodile heads for seats, we still wanted it to feel lived in. We wanted it to resemble an actual roadside attraction."

The production designers made subtle changes that added up to an overall shift in tone: They brought the walls in, installed booths, and took the sawdust off the floor. Nevertheless, the bar's proprietress, played by Beth Grant, is a strong personality, as shown in the scene where she finds Mad Sweeney drunk and collapsed in a men's room stall and proceeds to shoot a glass bottle out of his hand. The final design fit her character well—witty and with a sexy twang.

Early in production, Green and fellow showrunner Bryan Fuller were excited about developing this set, knowing that it needed to be surreal and over the top but without feeling manufactured. This dichotomy took a couple of tries to get right. Initially, they worked with illustrators to realize their vision on the page, and this guided the set builders. But when Fuller visited the set in person, he recalls having an upsetting realization: "I was like, 'Oh my God, this has to be redone, it doesn't work.' We were shooting the scene, and I'm having a conversation with Pablo about his role, and he's saying, 'Is this working for you?' And I'm thinking it doesn't matter because we're going to be reshooting this whole thing. In my head I was like, 'We've got to do something about this set.'"

They soon redesigned the set so that it looked less like a theme park attraction. "The original set for the bar was on the wrong side of nonreality," Green explains. "It felt unreal to a degree that made the strange events that took place there less believable. While we wanted a highly stylized place with crocodile teeth for

CZERNOBOG AND THE ZORYA SISTERS

"WHEN SHADOWS ARE LONG, THAT IS MY TIME. YOU ARE THE LONG SHADOW."

—ZORYA VECHERNYAYA, EPISODE 2

THE OLD GODS CZERNOBOG and the three Zorya sisters—Zorya Vechernyaya, Zorya Utrennyaya, and Zorya Polunochnaya— are poor gods, largely forgotten by the Slavic people who brought them over from the Old World. This poverty is clearly evident in episode 2 when we enter their Chicago apartment, which is the first time we see the intimate details of a god's home. As with many first-generation immigrants, their space is a time capsule of the land they left behind. From the lacy, Edwardian-era costumes to the cracked china and hand-rolled cigarettes, their apartment turns the clock back a full century and is permeated with the dreary cold winters of pre-Soviet Russia. "The first thing you meet when you get to the Zorya home is the apartment itself," executive producer Michael Green elaborates. "It's dank with decades of cigarette smoke yellowed into the walls. We come to learn that they've been here for quite some time, that they were part of a classic turn-of-the-century immigrant experience."

pieces and lawn furniture. One of my favorite bits was the blanket on Czernobog's bed. The buyer brought me beautiful embroidered period crests, and we attached them to a simple wool blanket."

Within these fading walls, the Zorya sisters and Czernobog fully articulate and embody the difficulty the Old Gods face in the New World. Their lives are not nice—gone are the trappings and devotions of their former glory, replaced by workaday drudgeries and an unending and unappreciated cosmic duty. They may once have been powerful and inspired fear and awe, but now they are nobodies, not even a nightmare. Thus, Wednesday's entreaty for them to join his war finds its mark relatively easily.

The production designer, Patti Podesta, went beyond Gaiman's description of the apartment in the book to bring it to life for the screen. "The Russians' apartment is described in the book as a small and dingy tenement. But I had in mind the distressed opulence of Robert Polidori's photographs of Cuban villas, which I thought could embody the backstory of the Russians, who would have come to the US in the twenties, lived in relative luxury, and now reside in simulacra. The crew and I bought historic wallpaper, applied it to the hallway, and then sanded it nearly away. The furniture is a mixture of period

Yet if their lives are diminished, that does not mean that their godly responsibilities are any less important. In particular, the three sisters are stars who watch over Ursa Minor, the constellation of the Little Bear in the night sky. Legend has it that a doomsday hound is chained to the star Polaris, and if the sisters ever pause in their vigilance, the hound will devour the constellation and the universe will end. "Everything said in the world of *American Gods* can be taken metaphorically and literally," Green explains. "When I hear a young woman on a rooftop say that she needs to keep an eye on the bear in

"There are similarities between Czernobog and Wednesday. But Czernobog's powers are much stronger; he is a complete god of destruction. That's why he has a twin brother—yin and yang. One brother is a complete destroyer and the other one is the rebuilder. It's like the famous passage in Ecclesiastes in the Bible, which goes something like: 'There's a time for everything under heaven. There is a time for war, there is a time for peace. There is time for chaos, there is time for tranquility' (Ecclesiastes 3). Czernobog works for Wednesday and he's loyal to Wednesday, but when Czernobog takes off on his own, it can cause mayhem in this world."

—Peter Stormare

the sky lest he destroy all creation, I believe her. And I think that her work is worth doing."

A FAMILY OF NECESSITY

AS OLD GODS, the Zorya sisters don't necessarily belong with Czernobog, who is akin to a Slavic Thor and god of darkness, after all. Yet necessity has driven them together. "He's nobody's husband," says Zorya Vechernyaya, played by the luminous Cloris Leachman, the Evening Star. "I'm nobody's wife. Family is who you survive with when you have to, even if you do not like them." These immigrant gods have been thrown together by circumstance, having come to America at the same time and brought by peoples with the same beliefs. "Neil chose to marry the Zorya sisters to Czernobog as a reluctant family," explains Green. "They're a family of necessity, being from the same larger region. The people who sang iterations of the same songs knew both their names."

It's understandable that Zorya Vechernyaya would want to distance herself from Czernobog. He's not a pleasant man. He seems to live off of cigarettes more than food or air, and he is perpetually drenched in the sweat and grime of his cow-killing labors. Peter Stormare, the actor cast as Czernobog, points out the benefit of the living arrangement to

"ZORYA POLUNOCHNAYA SEEMS TO WATCH SHADOW FROM THE MOMENT HE ENTERS THE APARTMENT. SHE DOESN'T INTERACT WITH MANY PEOPLE, MUCH LESS MANY MEN, SO THERE'S SOME CURIOSITY ABOUT THAT. BUT SHE'S ALSO A TOUCH PSYCHIC AND THAT MAKES HER WANT TO KNOW A BIT MORE ABOUT HIM. LIKE ALL OF THEM, SHE LIKES HIM, BUT SHE ISN'T IMPRESSED WITH HIM. SHADOW SEEMS TO GO ALONG WITH FAR TOO MUCH AT FACE VALUE."

: MICHAEL GREEN :
EXECUTIVE PRODUCER

his character. "I think the Zorya sisters just took him in," he explains. "Gods and demons are related in spirit, not in blood. As Thor, he could easily live in a rundown motel somewhere. But he's still alive because they care for him. They keep him alive." The four of them must coexist in this crumbling apartment, making do as contributing members of a family burdened with the needs and wants of modern life. Actress Erika Kaar, who plays Zorya Polunochnaya, the Midnight Star, explains, "These are gods, but they're also people who smoke cigarettes, who get hungry, who get fat during Christmas."

SHADOW'S DILEMMA

THE VISIT TO Czernobog and the Zorya sisters represents an early turning point for Shadow, who, since leaving prison days before, has been pummeled by a wide variety of supernatural occurrences and psychological traumas. He's begun to question his own sanity. And who wouldn't after meeting Mr. Wednesday, a magic-coin-wielding leprechaun, and a crazy toad-skin-vaping young man in the back of an otherworldly limo? The ground beneath Shadow's feet is not solid anymore: He is either hallucinating, or an unimaginably dangerous magic exists in the world. Neither alternative feels safe.

So when Czernobog proposes that Shadow risk his life on a game of checkers, he almost casually acquiesces.

"Vechernyaya takes an instant shine to Shadow. She refers to him as one of Wednesday's murderers, but she knows better. She can see—first by looking at him, and second by reading his fortune—that there's more to him than perhaps he even knows. Unfortunately, there's more to him than he might ever have a chance to find out because, given his apprenticeship to Wednesday, he may not live long enough to discover it."

—*Michael Green, executive producer*

"Shadow has begun engaging in a series of behaviors that could very well prematurely end his life," Green explains. "Part of Shadow seems willing to just cash it in, thinking maybe it is better to be dead than live in this terrifying world."

His predicament is understandable, if understated. A character as internal as Shadow can be hard to read, but given the context of his dilemma, it's easy to see how meaning and reason have taken a backseat in his mind. If none of this is real, and how could it be, why should it matter if Shadow loses his bet with Czernobog?

Thankfully, Zorya Polunochnaya arrives in what may or may not be a dream to give Shadow a glimmer of hope. Standing on her chilly Chicago rooftop, she pulls the moon from the sky and hands it to him in the form of a silver dollar coin, reminding him that he may yet have something to live for. "Shadow is on the verge of suicide," Kaar explains. "He wants Czernobog to kill him. Polunochnaya tries to teach him that even when life is shit—when you're in Chicago and you live with your sisters and eat only borscht every day—you still have to wake up and live."

As a result of Polunochnaya's intervention, Shadow realizes the world contains wonders he is only now glimpsing. But to survive, he needs to open his mind and stop disregarding the protections and blessings he is being offered.

EDWARDIAN ELEGANCE

THE THREE ZORYA sisters are suitably dressed in turn-of-the century Slavic fashion. Draped in high-necked, multi-layered frocks of cotton and lace, they look like painted figures who have stepped from a canvas into real life. Their frayed clothing may have a down-on-their-luck pall and appear a bit shabby, but they carry themselves with a regal poise.

Cloris Leachman, in particular, reveled in her character's wardrobe. Costume designer Suttirat Larlarb recalls, "She loved her coat and wanted to wear it all the time. She was so happy when she saw it. It was so intricate, with all this elaborate embroidery and fur detail." This love fueled Leachman's embodiment of her character and her air of faded aristocracy.

In real life, however, Leachman revealed a much bawdier side. Executive producer Bryan Fuller relates: "One of my favorite experiences with Cloris on the set was her turning ninety. We went to her trailer with this massive birthday cake, and she blew out the candles and said, 'Fuck me, I'm ninety.' Then she clarified, 'No, really, somebody fuck me.' Quite a character. She is a delight to work with."

BECOMING A STAR

PLAYED BY ACTRESS Martha Kelly, Zorya Utrennyaya is the Morning Star, and she does not speak, so we don't know much about her character. However, as the silent middle sister, she is a vigilant protectress of her younger sister. Kelly says, "Utrennyaya is there to protect the one sister who has to sleep all day and stay awake all night to keep watch against danger and supernatural things. She protects her from being woken up by those who are around during the day."

That nocturnal sister, Zorya Polunochnaya, is the youngest and most alluring of the three, though she was created by Gaiman and is not actually part of Slavic mythology. In the book, the Midnight Star bridges the gap between evening and dawn, and Gaiman imagined her as a sheltered young woman, a barefoot virgin who spends her nights alone on the rooftop, wrapped in a lace and cotton shift, watching the stars. Erika Kaar was advised, however, against basing her portrayal too literally on the book. "Even before I got the part," Kaar explains, "I read the book and looked at the stars and analyzed the constellations that you can see from Illinois, where I was working. But I was told not to get so obsessed with the book. The casting directors suggested that I be prepared and have my vision of the character and know as much about her as I could, but to draw a line between the book and the film itself."

Once the official shoot began, Kaar discovered this was good advice. "My idea of Zorya Polunochnaya was quite different from what she turned out to be in the end," Kaar explains. "I had this idea about her being from a different world and so delicate. Then when we started working on set, David Slade, the director, encouraged me to put more of her curiousness and a little bit of craziness out there. I think in the end we made her a little more weird than I thought she would have been." This touch of zaniness appeals to Kaar.

Kaar, a tomboy at heart, found that spirit came in handy during the shoot for the rooftop scene, which took place outside on a frigid night in Toronto. Kaar was dressed in a thin lace and cotton nightgown and not much else. In favor of authenticity, she chose to forgo even the most basic concessions. "I had to sacrifice my comfort to make her more true to herself," Karr explains. "Even though shooting in nothing but pajamas was quite uncomfortable, my character would never wear a bra in the middle of the night. I got all geeky about it. Even when we took half-body shots, and you couldn't see my legs, I would refuse to wear shoes. I would say, 'No, no. When you're barefoot, you move differently. I cannot wear those even though I am so cold.'"

thirty, made him indispensable. "In his long speech at dinner, when he challenges Shadow to a checkers game, he performed it thirty times, top-to-bottom," Green recalls. "One would think that would get boring, but we were captivated. It was a night shoot and went until very late, and he was riveting in every iteration of that performance on every angle. He brings joy into his work and a strange specificity to everything he does."

Perhaps the biggest challenge for the nonsmoking actor was the cigarettes, which Czernobog lights every chance he gets. This meant that, as Czernobog inhales deeply with the immense pleasure of a life-long smoker, Stormare was sucking down herbal cigarettes. "He is not by habit or disposition an actual smoker," Green explains. "He went through box after box of cigarettes. But between takes he would spit, chew gum, wash his mouth out, go 'Aggh! I hate it!'"

CZERNOBOG

CZERNOBOG STICKS IN one's mind like the smell of stale cigarette smoke, an aroma that clings to him even in sleep. He is an old and frustrated god, much reduced from the days when he could kill a man with a single blow from his sledgehammer. Now his bloodlust must be satisfied in the Chicago livestock killing yards, where modern technology has taken away the satisfaction of a good clean kill. Stormare sees Czernobog's dirty and disheveled state as evidence of his waning power. "He's fading away because no one pays him tribute anymore," he comments. "That's why Wednesday has come to him, to rekindle his lust to become a god again. He's reluctant to join because he has become addicted to his slovenly lifestyle of sitting on a couch, watching TV, drinking beer, eating popcorn and chips. Which is an American disease. I don't want to use the word 'lazy,' but it's like he's halfway to evaporating into nothingness."

"Czernobog manages to take grumpy and paint it in murderous colors," Green muses. "He's someone who, while everyone else enjoys their dinner, smokes rather than eats. He doesn't seem to need any nourishment other than the cigarettes he keeps pouring down his throat." In contrast, Peter Stormare, the actor who brings this grouchy chimney of a god to life, can't abide cigarettes, and he has been known to tote around a Hello Kitty backpack on set. The showrunners saw hundreds of audition tapes and considered a variety of actors for the role of Czernobog, but Stormare's performance went beyond what they had ever imagined. His range and commitment, whether on take four or take

"Czernobog is like the cab driver who was once a surgeon in his home country. Of course, he's the opposite of a surgeon. He's someone who can commit quite a bit of death."
—Michael Green, executive producer

Shadow saw a gray-haired old East-European immigrant, with a shabby raincoat and one iron-colored tooth, true. But he also saw a squat black thing, darker than the darkness that surrounded them, its eyes two burning coals; and he saw a prince, with long flowing black hair, and long black moustaches, blood on his hands and his face, riding, naked but for a bearskin over his shoulder, on a creature half-man, half-beast, its face and torso blue-tattooed with swirls and spirals.

—American Gods, *chapter 6*

The MYTHOLOGY of the BLACK GOD and the AURORA SISTERS

The mythological and cultural roots of Czernobog and the Zorya sisters are not the same, but they overlap. Czernobog arose among western Slavic tribes in the twelfth century, who believed that bad things happen in the world because of the "Black God." Historical records are slim, but Christian accounts of the time characterize Czernobog as a dark, accursed god, though his reputation among the Slavs may have been more nuanced. Regardless, bad luck, calamity, and misfortune were his hallmarks, and pagans of the time paid him heed, often by spitting curses at him in their bowls before dinner.

In Slavic mythology, the two Zorya sisters, Utrennyaya and Vechernyaya, have an important role in the workings of the heavens. Known as the Auroras, they open and close the gates of Dazbog's palace, letting the sun god traverse the skies during the day before locking him in again at night. They also watch over the doomsday hound that threatens to eat the constellation Ursa Minor. It was believed that if the hound's chain broke loose and the constellation were devoured, the universe would end. The third sister, Zorya Polunochnaya, is sometimes mentioned

in mythology, but Gaiman created the version that appears in the book. "Neil's take on the three sisters," Green explains, "is that, in addition to their day jobs of getting by in America, they still have a very important mythological job. Morning, noon, and night, they trade off sleeping and keeping an eye on the bear in the sky."

Erika Kaar grew up in Poland, so she feels a particular affinity for Slavic mythology, not to mention the Eastern European food that the Zorya sisters make—the strong, sweet coffee and the borscht with potatoes. All these elements rang true from her own childhood. To play the role of Polunochnaya, Kaar focused on what it would mean for a young woman with this background to live in modern-day Chicago. "I did research on the constellations, about the gods and where they came from," Kaar explains. "But I tried not to focus too much on the mythology because it takes away from the humanity of the character. I wanted to show the human, teenage aspects of Zorya. She is a goddess, but still part of her is just a long-haired girl discovering if it's worth it to talk to people, to make friends. Or are the stars better?"

"IS GOOD?"

—Czernobog, episode 2

TECHNICAL BOY

IN EPISODE 1, TECHNICAL Boy appears for the first time while vaping in the backseat of his limo, sporting sculpted hair, a red-and-white leather jacket, and a hacker's disregard for authority or pleasantries. He is the vanguard of the New Gods, the modern deities of technology, media, and globalization, who have been eclipsing the Old Gods in territory and devotees. Their march toward spiritual domination, converting people from faith in their heritage and traditions to slavish devotion to their iPads and televisions, has pushed Wednesday and his motley crew of gods and myths to go to war. Technical Boy, the youngest and most impulsive of the lot, seems to have more power and influence than he can handle.

Technical Boy's on-screen character is a far cry from his depiction in the book. As Neil Gaiman writes in chapter 2 of *American Gods:* "The fat young man at the other end of the stretch limo took a can of Diet Coke from the cocktail bar and popped it open. He wore a long black coat, made of some silky material, and he appeared barely out of his teens: a spattering of acne glistened on one cheek." On-screen, the young man sitting across from Shadow is more akin to a slick Silicon Valley hacker of the Instagram generation, supremely aware of his self-image and the need to stay ahead of the curve.

American Gods was published in 2001, and "the Technical Boy in the book comes from that era," comments executive producer Bryan Fuller. "Right after *The Matrix* and the fetishizing of leather trench coats and pseudo-hacker sexiness combined with the perception of overweight people in their basement who are socially stunted in some regard." Since then, technology has revolutionized society, privacy, fashion, media, and our sense of self. In the TV series, Technical Boy embodies these revolutions, displaying the cocky fashion and self-regard, smug technical fluidity, and innate insecurity that come with the territory. He's an extreme manifestation of our modern need for validation, embodying both the speed and disconnection of modern technology.

Actor Bruce Langley, who portrays Technical Boy, explains: "Tech Boy is a representation of the updating and expanding nature of technology and the Internet. There's an upgrade here, a new model there, everything is downloading all the time. He never has a moment to stop and find out what he is, where he lies, to get his bearings, and work out how he feels about anything because he's always focused on the next new thing, an external form of validation. He's got an unlimited supply of it, since he's the god of technology, so he's a victim of his own success."

BRIDGING THE TECHNOLOGICAL GAP

THOUGH TECHNICAL BOY'S appearance and manner have changed so that he is almost unrecognizable compared to who he is in the book, the character underscores how relevant Gaiman's writing remains. Technical Boy's importance and menace have only increased over the last fifteen-plus years, as technology and its risks have permeated every aspect of life. In the limo, Technical Boy gives an impassioned, dystopian

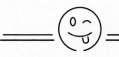

"THE CHILDREN ARE MY CRONIES. THEY ARE ESSENTIALLY DOWNLOADABLE HENCHMEN THAT I CAN REPLICATE AS MANY TIMES AS I WANT. THINK OF THEM AS FACELESS EXTENSIONS OF ME, A WALKING, SUBSERVIENT, HIVE MIND."

: BRUCE LANGLEY :

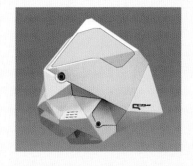

speech to Shadow, only slightly paraphrased from the book, showing the prescience of Gaiman's original ideas: "We have reprogrammed reality. Language is a virus. Religion is an operating system. Prayers are just so much fucking spam." More than ever, we know the debt we pay to the gods of technology, whether in the form of hard-earned cash for the latest iPhone or in time taken away from friendships and family for the pleasure of scrolling through an endlessly updating stream of social media. Technical Boy embodies these compromises, challenging what it once meant to be present in the world. Fuller explains: "We're in a world where people want to live presently as long as other people can see them and comment on their lives."

Langley admits that, when it came to depicting the character, he drew inspiration more from current events than from Gaiman's book: "People's perception and association with technology has changed exponentially in the past fifteen years. Today, it's Silicon Valley, Mark Zuckerberg, and this new, sexy, cutting-edge thing. Tech Boy is modern, he is ever changing, and anything based on the past he considers irrelevant. So by proxy of his own current character, no, I did not draw very much on the original basis of the character."

HIDDEN VULNERABILITIES

LANGLEY HAS A great time playing Technical Boy. "I'm a little bit in love with him," he says. "He's an absolute hoot to play with." One of the nuances that Langley brings to the role is an understanding of Technical Boy's vulnerabilities. Beneath that veneer of the cocky hacker, the character suffers from an extreme dislocation of self, which can affect anyone too absorbed in the unreal realm of technology. "He's an outsider," Langley explains. "In the ways that other people have learned to connect, he doesn't possess the same kind of social vocabulary.

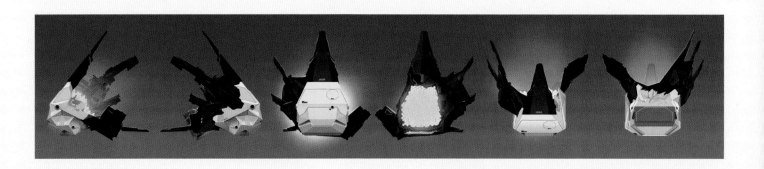

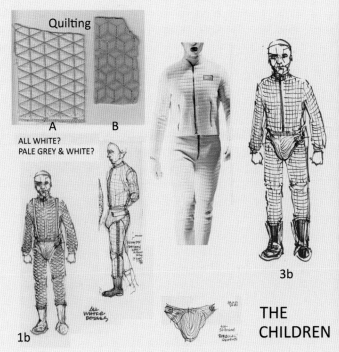

Quilting

A   B

ALL WHITE?
PALE GREY & WHITE?

1b

3b

THE
CHILDREN

He can't relate to people because he's semi-machine-brained—everything is binary. He just upgrades, and then he's not the same anymore, and he's got to reassess everything. Everyone else seems to get left behind because he thinks so much faster than them, but it makes him a lonely character."

This loneliness plays out in his relationship with some of the other gods, especially Bilquis, whom he sees as an easy target, manipulating her to bring her over to the side of the New Gods. "These very vindictive semi-abusive interactions he has with her," Langley explains, "when he's giving her missions and updating her on what's going to be happening, those are often the closest thing he has to human interaction. There may be a sliver of himself that enjoys having someone to talk to. The harsh truth is that the only people who will talk to him are people who have to talk to him or he will kill them."

GODFLESH

IN TECHNICAL BOY'S scene with Shadow in his limousine in the first episode, we see the first incarnation of an effect that the directors and VFX team pioneered, and sweated over, for the show. Shadow, after inhaling some second-hand toad

"We really pushed the creative envelope with our 'volumetric performance capture,' which we named godflesh. With Technical Boy we added lots of color in the re-skinning technique and really fell into the 'moving chiclets' animation after trying various forms crawling on his body."
—*Bernice Howes, VFX producer*

skin smoke from Technical Boy's vaping, is given the ability to see him in his true form, his "godflesh," as the showrunners came to call it. Chiclet-like tabs crawl over the surface of his head, transforming him into a digitized representation of himself. David Slade, the episode's director, elaborates on the effect: "Technical Boy's skin is crawling with blocks, tiny ticks of data and color that spin and fall, looking like he's made of Claymation, which Shadow sees as a kind of a hallucinatory experience." Like a character out of *Neuromancer*, that classic sci-fi novel of a dystopic technological future, Technical Boy's godflesh gives the lie to his otherworldly nature. He is as much an AI as he is human, a digital boy with a machine's capacity for data, learning, and cold calculation.

Each of the gods has a version of this godflesh, revealing their true power and appearance in its divine (and terrible) form. The behind-the-scenes technical process of research and discovery to achieve the effect was arduous, requiring the directors, directors of photography, and visual effects team to reach beyond presently available technology. The result is both visually convincing and adaptable within the particular structure of a television shooting schedule.

Slade realized early on that making the godflesh effect using traditional 3D computer graphic technology was too expensive and time-consuming for a television production, even one with a large budget. He also wanted an effect that didn't rely on animation to achieve it, and that would even go beyond traditional motion-capture technologies. Those processes require careful planning to achieve a shoot that is more about enabling the technology—actors are covered with tiny sensors called witness cameras to capture their movements, which are then used by the animators to translate into CG—than about working within the multiple-take process of an on-the-ground television shoot. He wanted to work with the performances he was able to capture from the actors when they were at their best and then manipulate the footage to achieve a look that is a close cousin to animation, without the compromises and schedule restrictions of that art form. "I've come across this problem with animation before," Slade elaborates. "When you animate things they go out of the real human world and into a world of magic, which can be wonderful if you're entirely in that world, but sometimes the two pieces don't fit. So I tasked my visual department to find a way to photograph an actor and automatically take that photography and turn it into a three-dimensional mesh. So there are no choices to be made by an animator—what you see is what you get."

The system Slade came up with was an array of cameras that photographed the actors at various angles, which allowed him to extract data that could then be translated into the automatic mesh. That mesh could essentially act as a filter on the performance, enabling the VFX team to manipulate its appearance, without having to actually animate the performance. "We would photograph an actor in three dimensions to create what we call a "Point Cloud" of the performance," Slade explains. "Then we could capture the little twitch in his eye, the spatial distance between the way he grins and the way he smiles. With that data, we can re-skin it in another kind of flesh."

THE FASHION GOD

TECHNICAL BOY HAS by far the greatest number of costume changes in the show, appearing in a different fantastical outfit in every scene. This reflects the close modern relationship between fashion and technology, and costume designer Suttirat Larlarb wanted to make sure that, for a character who is constantly upgrading, no two looks would be the same. Larlarb says, "Tech Boy needs to feel like the character who has the fastest, most expendable fashion. Items that are insanely expensive, visually disposable, but very striking in the moment. Most important is the irreverence of it. Even if it reeks of money and status, it needs to be irreverent in its expression. He would never repeat anything twice."

Langley concurs, and this is partly why his character's depiction goes so far beyond the book. In the show, Technical Boy wears cutting-edge fashion trends that are happening right now or are about to happen. Technology has pushed what is possible in fashion, from new fabrics to new manufacturing techniques. For example, in episode 1, Technical Boy wears an orange mesh integration that is relatively space age. In episode 8 he's in an LED jacket—the fibers light up. "A lot of Tech Boy's costumes would not have been possible to create even ten years ago," Langley explains. "The technology used in things like the fabric weaving literally did not exist. I shudder to think of the amount of money that I was walking around in. It's all a reflection of him constantly changing and upgrading."

Though much of Technical Boy's look is forward leaning, there are some throwback references. The interior of his limo, in particular, is a nod to the Commodore 64, the popular 1982 8-bit home computer. "The main thing about Commodore 64," comments Langley, "was that you could transmit software patches virally. You didn't need to get any special pieces of hardware to rewrite programming and share it. So people could essentially pirate programming, which allowed for a massive exchange of information. It was the early true nerd's hack-way into gaming and computers and all the rest of it."

Almost as much as his clothes, Technical Boy's hair provided fertile creative ground, in this case for lead hair designer Karola Dirnberger and her team. His hair had to be as futuristic in style as his clothes, and change just as often. "Tech Boy is supposed to look like he prints himself in a 3D printing machine," Dirnberger elaborates, "so his hair has to be perfect. But he is also the kind of guy who would see a style on someone out on the street and think it's cool. But when he prints it, it doesn't come out exactly right. It's always a little bit off."

"Technical Boy spends some of his time around large groups of people, which may be to bolster his ego. But people are something that either he doesn't understand or he's worked them out to a point where they're completely uninteresting. However, there is still a part of him that is slightly human. His conflict is that, 'I know they think so many quadrillion cycles slower than me. It's insulting to even share the same air as them. However, I still need some form of connection because part of me is still a little bit human.'"

—Bruce Langley

Technical Boy, episode 8

Worship is a volume business.

PART TWO

THE COMING WAR

> "I'M THE IDIOT BOX. I'M THE TV. I'M THE ALL-SEEING EYE AND THE WORLD OF THE CATHODE RAY. I'M THE BOOB TUBE. I'M THE LITTLE SHRINE THE FAMILY GATHERS TO ADORE."
> —MEDIA, *AMERICAN GODS*, CHAPTER 7

LIKE TECHNICAL BOY, THE character of Media has only become more relevant and frightening for today's audiences. Media embodies our modern media culture, with twenty-four-hour cable news channels, on-demand programming, series binge watching, and the recent blossoming of "fake news." We have more viewing options than ever before, and more ways to consume them, but more information and entertainment does not make us better, smarter people. We depend on media for our opinions, political identities, and values, and yet we also mistrust it, and this is fertile ground for Media. Since *American Gods* was written, American society has become exactly what the Media of the book would have hoped for: People are spoon-fed ideas and values, and they rarely question whether these are valid, worthwhile, or wise. Actress Gillian Anderson, who plays Media, immediately recognized how today's media consumption would benefit her character. "Since Neil wrote this book," she explains, "there's been a cumulative impact of media on us as human beings. We don't have role models or iconic characters that we are obsessed with anymore. The point is more the degree of our obsession as measured by the escapism that it provides."

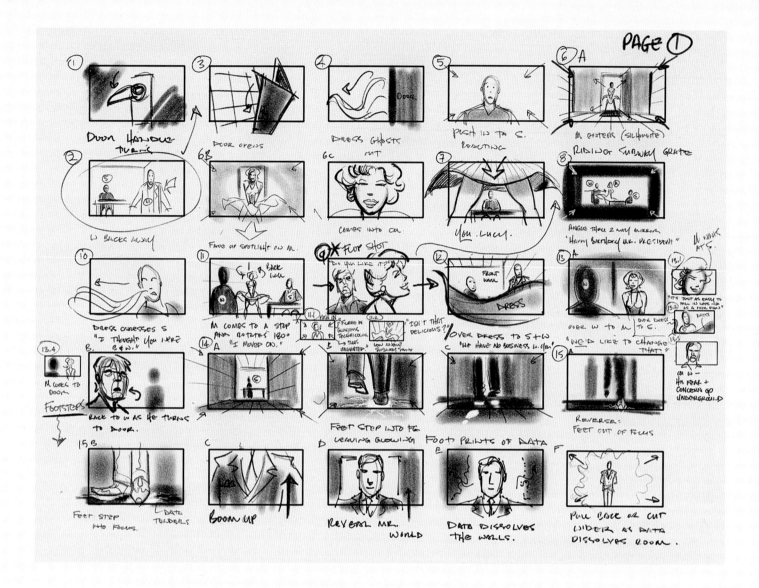

In order to play Media, one of the cold and conniving New Gods, Anderson also has to become Lucille Ball (as Lucy Ricardo), Judy Garland, Marilyn Monroe, and David Bowie. Media channels herself through these four iconic figures, using their star power to manipulate the world around her. Anderson gives a striking performance, bringing a multilayered approach to each character. But finding the balance between the calculating Media and these larger-than-life personalities was a particular challenge. "Media was tricky to figure out," Anderson explains. "She shows up as several iconic characters, and my approach for how best to have her personality come through changed every time. There was fun in the process of disappearing into them and messing with whomever it is she's talking to."

For Lucille Ball, the first character Anderson filmed, she had to feel her way toward the right level of impersonation. Anderson watched *I Love Lucy* videos to master the lilt of Ball's voice and quirks, to which Anderson added Media's steely presence. At first, what resulted wasn't quite what Anderson was looking for. "I started working on voices, attitudes, and physicality," Anderson recalls. "And then I realized that if I brought Lucy in too much in the voice, it sounded weird because none of the things that I was saying were things that Lucy would say. It was distorted. I decided that Lucy should have a healthy dose of Media and of the monotone, plowing-through of information that she does to get what she wants, with a tinge of Lucy's voice."

Judy Garland posed a similar challenge. "With Judy," Anderson explains, "I found that any time I started to force her voice, or mimic that particular smile that she had, it started to take away from Media's underlying menace."

"In the Marilyn Monroe scene, she knows that Mr. World is the boss in the room, so she's not having to do all the work. She's one of the side characters in that scenario. Since she's not the primary manipulator, it was easier for her to be splashy and flirty as Marilyn."

—Gillian Anderson

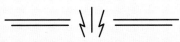

would resonate more with modern audiences, and they knew Anderson had the range to pull off a variety of personalities. If updating Technical Boy meant changing his wardrobe, then updating Media meant expanding her avatars so they captured a broader spectrum of iconic twentieth-century figures in order to express the full range of Media's influence and power.

BECOMING MEDIA (AND LUCY, JUDY, MARILYN, AND BOWIE)

COMING UP WITH the right costumes for Media and her many characters was no small feat. Each look had to be instantly recognizable and yet still work within the overall aesthetic and context of the show. "Suttirat Larlarb had such a clear vision," Anderson explains. "She and Bryan knew what elements they wanted to pull from the original costumes worn by these characters, which they mixed with modern, futuristic elements. It would even come down to particular colors, like a particular type of pink."

Costume designer Larlarb had fun with the challenge. "Gillian is a stunningly beautiful person, so she's a pleasure to dress," she recalls. For Marilyn, whom Gillian asked to be added to the show, the choice was simple: They used the white dress she wears in *The Seven Year Itch,* the one that billows up revealingly as she stands over a subway grate, which has become one of the best-known moments in twentieth-century cinema. As with Lucy, Gillian also mimics the famous lilt of Marilyn's voice, somehow managing to make it sexy and creepy at the same time. The effect is mesmerizing. "The leaps that she made with Marilyn Monroe were impressive," Fuller explains. "She crafted that representation so pitch-perfectly

STAYING TRUE TO THE SCRIPT

WITH GRACE AND style, Anderson slips seamlessly into each role, while the costumes, hair, and makeup help bring each to life. This apparent ease took a lot of study. Anderson watched hours of video and film of each performer to capture their habits, voices, and gestures. The one thing she didn't study was the book. "With real-life characters, you pull from history," Anderson says. "But with literary characters, sometimes I find adhering to the book can be a disservice to the creative process. I allow the world of the teleplay to be the most important. With Bryan's writing and Neil's input, I had complete faith that what they created has everything they want to present to the audience."

At times, Anderson couldn't help but rely on the teleplay, considering how much the showrunners changed Media for the series. In the book, Media becomes a handful of personalities: for instance, Lucille Ball's Lucy Ricardo, a newswoman, and Diane from *Cheers.* But Green and Fuller wanted characters who

that, when I watched the scene in dailies, my jaw was on the ground."

Media as Marilyn's scene in episode 5 opens with her floating into the interrogation room where Shadow and Wednesday are held captive, her iconic dress fluttering about her legs as though blown by an otherworldly breeze. Creating this levitating, breezy Marilyn was a technical challenge—the skirt of the dress was shown at a slower frame rate, giving it the look of perpetual slow-motion. Vincenzo Natali, the episode's director, recalls the process: "For all intents and purposes, it is a practical effect. Originally, we wanted to do the dress digitally, but that was cost-prohibitive. So we photographed all of Marilyn's shots at minus-six frames per second and then we sped up everything but the dress and digitally painted the slow dress into a twenty-four-frame shot. It was a tricky business—all the hard work was left to the post-production team."

Media's other characters do not have a single defining look or wardrobe choice that stands out from their long careers. "For Lucy," Larlarb continues, "I tried to amalgamate lots of different Lucy looks in one costume. We needed something to pack a punch right away. Black-and-white polka dots felt right for the fifties vibe." The fact that Lucy's scene is filmed in black and white created an opportunity for the makeup department, who rarely get to work in that medium. "When something's in black and white it affords me a great deal more license in terms of reshaping the face," Colin Penman, head of makeup, comments. "You can use colors that just wouldn't look that great in full color—they'd be too stark or contrasted." The black-and-white scene does flash to color at one moment, and Penman admits that he's pretty critical of how Lucy's makeup looks at that moment. "When I see it I think, 'Those are some strong colors going on there.'" But it's just a moment in an otherwise gorgeous sequence. And like most artists, Penman is likely his own worst critic.

Media appears as David Bowie in episode 5, joining Technical Boy in the stretch limo. In this scene they wanted Media to be graphically jarring, cool, and wildly futuristic, so they chose Bowie's Ziggy Stardust persona, decking Anderson out in blue eyeshadow, a spiky red mullet, and a turquoise suite. "Bowie is so widely different from the other characters Media appears as across the series," Fuller comments. "None of the other versions of Media are in trousers, which plays up the androgyny. I wanted her to feel electric, to convey a sense that Technical Boy is the emperor of the digital era and Media is looking back across the twentieth century."

Nailing the Bowie look was a challenge for everyone involved, including lead hair designer Karola Dirnberger. "It took me three wigs to get the color, shape, everything just right," she comments. "It's amazing how different hair looks on camera than it does to the human eye. So for the first wigs, I was not happy with the color at all. When you're doing work like this, where you're mimicking someone who actually lived, you want it to be perfect. God's in the details. Or, in this case, the American Gods are in the details."

Shooting this scene was more than a wardrobe challenge, particularly for Anderson. As often happens, the shoot was running behind schedule, and Anderson had been waiting for almost three hours in full hair and makeup before she finally got on set. Then, the limo was constructed to retract over the actors, encasing them inside. "I had to sit in the back of the limo in my suit and hair and shoes," Anderson recalls. "They shut the door and taped me in, and it was about 150 degrees in there. Between that and the smoke, which was drying out my voice, and the fact that there was nowhere to hide a bottle of water. . . I could just manage to sit on a fan between takes so that I could have some air." In the end, nary a hint of discomfort is evident on Anderson's pristinely pale face.

"I remember talking to Ricky Whittle, and he was saying, 'Why Judy Garland? Nobody knows who Judy Garland is!' And I said, 'If they don't, they should, and maybe they'll look her up after they see the season finale because Judy Garland is punk rock.'"
—*Bryan Fuller, executive producer*

In season 1's final episode, Media appears while escorted by a multiplying entourage of faceless Children in Fred Astaire–style suits. Who is she now? Those not up on their mid-twentieth-century musicals might need to do a little Googling: She's Judy Garland in the role of Hannah Brown from the movie *Easter Parade*, which costars Fred Astaire. While the showrunners might have picked Garland's iconic portrayal of Dorothy in *The Wizard of Oz*, the context of the scene and the relationship of the characters drove the choice. Media arrives at the house of Easter, one of the Old Gods, on Easter Sunday, so of course she would embody a famous performer from a movie featuring Easter.

"Garland is so raw and vulnerable and powerful and irrepressible as a performer, that to take her character from *Easter Parade* was a pop culture connection that we couldn't resist," Fuller explains. "It's Easter, she's celebrating Easter, so she's cosplaying for her good friend in a role from a film that they might have enjoyed together at some point in their histories. It also gave us an interesting opportunity to elaborate on a genuine friendship between an Old God and a New God. We've got some interesting places to go with Easter and Media in the future and how their relationship will be tested from either side of their respective teams. Something fun for us to look forward to unpacking in season 2."

"WE WANT TO HELP YOU FIND YOUR AUDIENCE."

—Media, episode 5

SALIM & THE JINN

> "THE OLD BELIEVE. THEY DO NOT PISS INTO HOLES. BECAUSE THE PROPHET TOLD THEM THAT JINN LIVE IN HOLES. THEY KNOW THAT THE ANGELS THROW FLAMING STARS AT US WHEN WE TRY TO LISTEN TO THEIR CONVERSATIONS. BUT EVEN FOR THE OLD, WHEN THEY COME TO THIS COUNTRY WE ARE VERY, VERY FAR AWAY."
> —THE JINN, EPISODE 3

LAURA ISN'T THE ONLY person chasing a lover across the country in *American Gods*. Salim, an immigrant salesman from Oman, chases a jinn, a supernatural creature from Islamic mythology, from New York City to Kentucky, falling in with Laura and Mad Sweeney along the way.

Though Salim and the Jinn appear relatively briefly in the first season—the Jinn is seen for a moment in passing in episode 2 their romantic meeting occurs in episode 3, and then Salim accompanies Mad Sweeney and Laura on part of their journey in episode 6—they are two of the more memorable characters in season 1.

> "Salim's suit doesn't fit, which was an accident in costume. I had lost some weight from the fitting to when we started shooting, and they were like, 'Wow, it doesn't fit you anymore.' I was like, 'Well, I don't think anything fits for him anyway, so it actually works great.'"
> —*Omid Abtahi*

THE UNHAPPY SALESMAN

UNLIKE MANY OF the other mortals in *American Gods* who are seeking answers or questioning their role in the world, the one problem that Salim does not possess is a crisis of faith. When we first meet him he is a fish out of water, a Middle Eastern salesman in an ill-fitting suit plying his wares in the dank and inhospitable import/export offices of Manhattan. He seems doomed to failure on every level—even the weather turns against him with a sudden downpour—when he steps into a taxicab and meets his driver, a fellow Arab. They strike up a conversation until the driver reveals his true nature, when Salim catches a glimpse of the flames that flicker where his eyes should be. In a moment that most would meet with panic—a flame-eyed taxi driver would terrify even the most jaded New Yorker—Salim seems to greet it with an open mind, perhaps even feeling at ease for the first time in this strange land. As it turns out, this Jinn is as familiar and real to him as the rain falling from the sky. He is a central character from Islamic mythology, a creature as essential to Salim's belief as Noah and his Ark are to any Bible school–educated child of Christianity. Salim readily shows that he does not need to find his faith; he already believes in the full power and mystery of Islam, and this taxi–driver Jinn is simply that belief incarnate. The ease with which Salim accepts the appearance of this Old God puts Shadow's constant crisis of faith into stark relief. The ensuing affair between Salim and the Jinn reveals the power that lies in

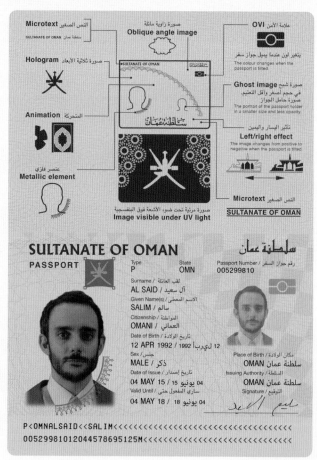

unquestioning belief, and is one of the most intimate and resonant scenes of pleasure and connection in the show.

Omid Abtahi, the actor cast to play Salim, found much he could relate to in the unhappy salesman. "I fell in love with Salim after the first read-through," he comments. "I fell in love with the idea of playing a character who has probably lived his whole life with a certain amount of shame. He didn't feel that he was allowed to love himself or who he was. I wanted to show the beauty and love of being a gay man as well as the beauty and love of Islam." Abtahi's journey to the heart of the character began with the source material. Unlike some of his fellow cast members who preferred not to be strongly influenced by the original work, Abtahi looked to Gaiman's book as a source of truth. "To me it was important to read the blueprint that Gaiman laid out and be adaptable enough to have my own interpretation of it. It spoke to me on my first

"PEOPLE BONDED TO THESE TWO CHARACTERS BECAUSE THEY MIGHT BE THE MOST RELATABLE CHARACTERS IN THE SHOW. THEY'RE JUST SEEKING SOME SORT OF CONNECTION. EVERYBODY ELSE IS TRYING TO GET SHADOW TO BELIEVE. BUT HERE YOU HAVE SALIM, WHO ALREADY DOES BELIEVE AND IS READY TO GIVE HIMSELF OVER TO THAT BELIEF."

: OMID ABTAHI :

read-through and it doesn't always happen like that as an actor. When you're adapting what's considered great literature, you want to give 110 percent and make sure you're truthful to the original content."

LOVING JINN

WHEN SALIM AND the Jinn arrive at the salesman's hotel room, they engage in a sensual, emotional, and definitely NSFW act of love. While sex scenes between men on television are no longer the taboo they were even a decade ago, the fact that this one is between two Middle Eastern men, one of them a jinn, pushes some additional cultural boundaries. To its credit, however, the power of the scene does not lie in its social or political impact. In a series that is in large part about our struggle to believe and connect with the larger forces in our lives—our history, our faith, our love—as is embodied by the journeys of Shadow

and Laura, the love story of the Jinn and Salim is a touching example of human connection and the gifts that we give to each other through physical intimacy and acceptance.

Mousa Kraish, the actor cast as the Jinn, sees his character as eminently relatable, despite his supernatural nature. "The Jinn seems to be the most human out of all the gods," he comments. "He's been here for so long, but he doesn't expect any worship from anybody. To meet someone on a lonely night and have a connection, that's all he is looking for. We've all felt lonely and out of place—that's what I was connecting to as an actor." When he first learned that he would need to be nude for the scene, Kraish had some concerns about the intentions behind the material. But Fuller and Green reassured him that the scene was not included in the episode for shock value. This focus on the intimacy and humanity of the relationship between the Jinn and Salim, rather than on the sensational aspect of their lovemaking, paid off. "I haven't heard a negative reaction to that scene," Kraish comments. "It's about two people who have a pure, unfiltered connection with one another. It's that simple. I want to show pure love—that two men can love one another. Whatever sexuality you are, whoever is watching this, I want you to see two people connecting."

Abtahi had a similar take on the scene from Salim's point of view. "To me, the physical sex act was a way for these two souls to share in this experience," he explains. "That's why when I read the part, as graphic as it sounds when the Jinn shoots his semen inside and you can see it go up into Salim's eyes, I was

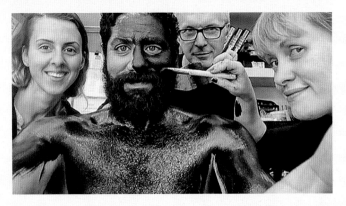

like, 'Wow, I really hope they keep this.' Because when two people have sex, they become one. And that was a moment where they were almost like one being of fire."

MAKEUP MISHAPS

ONE SURPRISING ISSUE that came up when filming the hotel room scene was not the nudity or intimacy that it demanded, but rather the makeup that the actors had to wear. The shiny black skin that the Jinn and Salim acquire during the scene was not achieved solely with VFX. It is real, greasy makeup—a cosmetic charcoal powder mixed with baby oil—covering them from head to toe. On-screen it gives them an otherworldly look, perfect for a sex scene with an Islamic spirit. On set, however, the makeup was messy and unpredictable since it readily came off the skin and onto any surface it touched. Though it didn't matter if the makeup transferred between the actors during their moments of intimacy, it did matter that it transferred to the white sheets on the bed. "The set dressers had a technique to deal with it," explains Colin Penman, head of makeup. "The sheets were folded back so that every few takes, they pulled the sheet away and then there was another fresh one underneath."

Cleanup was a bit unorthodox as well. "Getting the makeup off was hilarious," Penman continues. "Oil and water—they don't mix. We were literally in the shower in Mousa's trailer with me scrubbing him. We became quite close that day."

TRANSFORMATION

AFTER HIS ENCOUNTER with the Jinn, Salim goes through a transformation akin to Laura's change from despondent wife to devoted lover, though without the inconvenience of being dead. He evolves from a lost young man, clinging to his job and place in life without conviction, to a fully realized and confident individual, traveling across the country in single-minded pursuit of the Jinn. However, whereas Laura is completely faithless, relying on her own pluck, smarts, and determination to get by, Salim is the embodiment of faith, giving himself over completely to the new life he has gained from his encounter with the Jinn. "Salim is able to ground Laura and show by example what it's like to have faith," Abtahi explains. "He shows her what faith means, and the beauty of faith as opposed to the negative aspects. When you see Salim in episode 6, he is very grounded and self-assured, in contrast to Laura, who's struggling with who she is."

The question that viewers are left with in episode 6, as Salim turns his taxi toward the horizon after Laura and Mad Sweeney take their leave to continue following Shadow and Mr. Wednesday, is, why is he chasing the Jinn? What more does he desire from the mysterious ifrit? Carnal pleasure? Or is he himself now part Jinn, having consumed some of the fire from the Jinn's eyes? "I asked Bryan and Michael this question," Abtahi reveals. "What does Salim want from the Jinn? Is it just more sex? Or is he seeking enlightenment? And Bryan's answer, which I agree with, was that it is a combination of all those things. This is probably the first time in his life that Salim has connected in a pure form to another human being. I think if anyone reflects on their own life and the times that we've connected to people that we hardly know, we have a desire to follow them where they go."

"**M**y grandmother swore that she had seen an ifrit, or perhaps a marid, late one evening, on the edge of the desert. We told her that it was just a sandstorm, a little wind, but she said no, she saw its face, and its eyes, like yours, were burning flames."

—Salim to the Jinn,
American Gods, *chapter 7*

The MYTHOLOGY of the JINN

"In my mind, the Jinn is pre-Islamic, he's pre-religion," Kraish explains when asked about the origins of his character. "When I was growing up, my parents told me stories about jinn and how they walk in a different world than we do. They can see us, but we can't see them unless they reveal themselves. We don't see them as genies. They don't grant wishes. They are another being that God has created. Humans were made out of clay, angels were made out of light, and jinns he made from fire. They're not demons, but like my mom would say, 'There's good jinn and then there's bad jinn.'"

The Jinn in *American Gods* would, it seems, agree with this assessment. "They know nothing about my people here," the Jinn says, speaking of the Americans that he drives around in the back of his taxi. "They think all we do is grant wishes. If I could grant a wish, do you think I would be driving a cab?"

In essence, jinn are supernatural creatures with roots dating back to pre-Islamic times. They are mentioned in early Arabian mythology as well as throughout the Quran, where they are included in the four categories of sapient creations of God: jinn, demons, humans, and angels. As Islam spread throughout the Middle East and Persia, the jinn began to take on the forms and powers of spirits, fairies, and deities of other cultures, such as in the story of "The Fisherman and the Jinni" in *One Thousand and One Nights*. In these stories jinn are sometimes able to fly, travel instantaneously from one place to another, or grant wishes. While entertaining, these aspects are considered to be fictional since within Islamic tradition jinn are regarded as part of the concrete world. "I don't know any Middle Eastern kid who doesn't believe in jinn," Kraish comments. "They're sort of the equivalent of ghost stories. Once when I was in Jordan I saw a jinn. I saw an old man with goat's legs out of the corner of my eye. I swear it to this day. I was on the beach and we found a really huge odd-looking snake-skin, and then underneath a dead tree, I saw this old man, but when I looked back he was gone. I swear that was a jinn."

Anansi

The *Coming to America* vignette that prefaces the second episode, "The Secret of Spoons," is one of the most affecting, and culturally relevant, scenes in the series. It launches the journey of Anansi, a.k.a. Mr. Nancy, an African trickster god of knowledge and stories, who travels to America aboard a slave ship. We are first introduced to him in spider form, crawling along the rafters and listening to the prayers of one of the shackled men, who is begging for freedom, truth, and justice of any kind. Mr. Nancy soon appears in his human form and gives a galvanizing speech that speaks not only to the predicament of the men on the boat but to African Americans today:

"You all get to America, land of opportunity, milk and honey, and guess what? You all get to be slaves! Split up, sold off, and worked to death. The lucky ones get off Sunday to sleep and fuck and make more slaves for them to work. And all for what? For cotton? Indigo? For a fucking purple shirt? The only good news is the tobacco your kids are gonna farm for free is gonna give a shitload of them white motherfuckers cancer. And I haven't even started yet. A hundred years later? You're fucked. A hundred years after that? Fucked. A hundred years after you get freed, you're still getting fucked out a job and shot at by police. See what I'm saying?"

The slaves on the ship may not get all three of the things they are asking for—though Anansi delivers truth in his description of the reality the men will face in Colonial America, and justice by inciting them to fight back, the freedom that comes in death pales in comparison to the freedom left behind on their native shores. Once the men decide what to do with the little power that they have left (plus a little divine help in loosening their shackles) they quickly set fire to the boat, dooming themselves and their captors to a watery grave.

During filming, when Orlando Jones, the actor who plays Mr. Nancy, gave this monologue, he captivated everyone on set with his exceptional delivery, which is full of a preacher's cadence and a performer's command of the stage. "When we filmed that sequence," executive producer Bryan Fuller recalls, "we had a room full of thirty black actors listening to his speech about the black man's experience in America—the entire set erupted in applause. At that moment we realized we might be striking a nerve with the tales that we're telling."

Jones agrees, saying, "In the historical context of being an African American in the United States and in the context of the political times that we live in, we found ourselves with a rare opportunity to bring those sorts of words to life. Television generally shies away from content that has that sort of gravitas."

In the episode, as the slave ship burns and sinks into the ocean (and Mr. Nancy, back in his spider form, rides to shore on a piece of the wreck), the scene cuts to Shadow hanging from a tree, surrounded by the Children, a group of faceless white men who evoke a lynch mob. The juxtaposition brings home the message of Mr. Nancy's speech and shows him to be a god who speaks truth to power.

> "Lemme tell you a story. 'Once upon a time a man got fucked.' How's that for a story? 'Cause that's the story of black people in America."
>
> —Mr. Nancy, episode 4

"A lot of the slave ship scene is visual effects designed not to look like visual effects. Like the slow rocking we added so that you get the feeling you're on a boat, though the scene was shot on a set that was built on solid land."
—*David Stump, VFX supervisor*

"We didn't get around to shooting the burning ship until the last day of the shoot. Since we inserted the burning ship in the sequence using VFX, we had to approach it like part of a three-dimensional puzzle. Months earlier we pulled the set pieces out that were meant to burn and positioned them in the parking lot. When you pick up the whole set and move it, it's easy to lose track of the relative camera positions and focal lengths, which need to match up. So I sprayed the camera marks on the ground, measured out so that we could get back to it again."
—*David Stump, VFX supervisor*

MR. NANCY

> "YOU ALREADY DEAD, ASSHOLE. AT LEAST DIE A SACRIFICE FOR SOMETHING WORTHWHILE. LET THE MOTHERFUCKER BURN! LET IT ALL BURN!"
>
> —ANANSI, EPISODE 2

"**I AM WHAT YOU MIGHT** consider a psycho *American Gods* fan," Orlando Jones says. Jones read the book long before the series was even a twinkle in Bryan Fuller's and Michael Green's eyes, and he became a regular in *American God* chat rooms. He even developed an ongoing conversation with author Neil Gaiman via Twitter. Then, early in the show's development, fans online suggested that Jones be cast as Mr. Nancy, which he didn't take seriously until he received a phone call from the casting directors. "When the call came in," Jones recalls, "I looked at the phone like, 'Are you reading this off the Internet? Is this a prank?' That was completely surreal to have seen a suggestion for me to play a role cross my feed and then have it come to fruition in real life." Accepting the role did interrupt his life as a fan, however. Jones soon realized that he couldn't participate in the chat rooms and fan conversations anymore. Now he knew too much, and he couldn't share any of it.

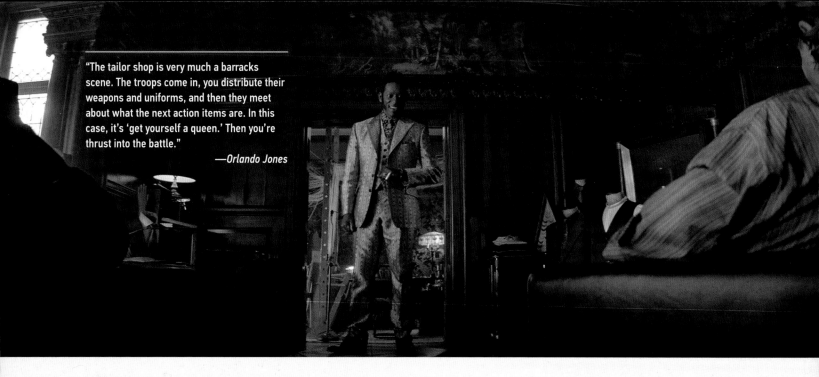

Jones recognizes the supreme challenge of adapting *American Gods* for television, and he has been duly impressed by Fuller and Green. The *Coming to America* slave ship scene, for example, does not appear in the book, but it frames the essence of Mr. Nancy and embodies the high aims of the series. "To play that role in this series in these times is for me one of the high points of my career," he explains. "Bryan and Michael did tremendous work drafting the two major speeches that Mr. Nancy

gives about the role of people of color and the role of women in this society. Two disenfranchised groups that are fighting for their rights today, just as they were many moons ago. It was a distinct honor for me to be able to bring that character to life."

A TRICKSTER GOD

WHEN WE MEET Mr. Nancy on the slave ship, he impresses everyone with his passion and wisdom; he speaks difficult truths and gives voice to the voiceless. The truth is, though, that he also leads those poor souls to commit suicide. Due to Mr. Nancy's persuasive oratory, the slaves go from subdued and chained to enraged and murderous in a few short minutes. This is Mr. Nancy's power. He uses words to manipulate others into doing what he thinks is right, no matter the consequences. It's a tricky thing to ask someone else to die for a noble cause they believe in while you politely crawl off the boat.

"Mr. Nancy uses language to trap, trick, and manipulate those around him," Jones elaborates. "That's the origin of the character. The spider—it's not like a lion. It's a very vulnerable creature, so it relies on its cunning to survive. I think that's what really drew me to the character. He's mercurial; you're never quite sure if he believes in what he's telling you."

YOU NEED A QUEEN

IN THE EIGHTH and final episode of season 1, Mr. Nancy uses the same verbal prowess to guide Shadow and Mr. Wednesday at a crucial juncture in their journey. The duo have just taken the head of Vulcan, a powerful Old God who had been coopted by the New Gods, in what is their first active move in their war against the New Gods. Now they are on their way to meet Easter, who is in a similar compromised position, but first they must purchase Easter suits. As they wait in Mr. Nancy's tailor shop, they are more exposed than at any other time, literally so, since they are sitting in their underwear and bathrobes. That Mr. Nancy is splendidly dressed only underscores their vulnerability.

Mr. Nancy knows two things: first, that Shadow does not understand what he's gotten himself into, and second, that the war they are pursuing has no guarantee of victory. Wednesday may be Odin, the king of the Old Gods, but he is prone to recklessness and chaos. He is tumbling ill-prepared toward war with a confused mortal who is making a mess of things along the way. Mr. Wednesday needs advice, and Mr. Nancy steps in to help steer him toward victory. "You better get yourself a queen!" he says. "'Cause you just went and killed one of theirs." And, as he told the slaves on the slave ship, you need to get angry.

Orlando Jones appreciates what Mr. Nancy says and his persuasive power. "Nancy utilizes the very things that minority groups are often maligned for," he explains. "Their power, intelligence, cleverness. Powerful women are often 'bitches,' whereas powerful men are described as 'cunning.'" By telling Wednesday that he needs to find himself a queen, Mr. Nancy promises the show's audience something that is lacking in the book *American Gods:* He signals that the women in the story—including mortals, undead, and gods—will be the equals of their male counterparts. As executive producer Bryan Fuller explains, "There is a shortage of substantial female characters in the book, and we wanted to change that, to embrace the women who were leaping out at us, especially Bilquis, Laura, and Media."

DRESSING A TAILOR

MR. NANCY IS a tailor who makes webs, both with words and with spider threads, weaving his way forward through history. The character originated in West African folklore and has a long history in the American South, and his costume needed to bring together many colorful elements. For Mr. Nancy's suit on the slave ship, costume designer Suttirat Larlarb turned to materials and dyes that would have been available at the time, including indigo and cotton. She worked with Jones to determine the palette, specifically the use of purple to denote his stature as a god and a range of colors inspired by the nomadic tribes of Ghana, West Africa, and the Caribbean.

In the novel, Gaiman describes Mr. Nancy as wearing a pair of yellow gloves, but these were put aside. They distracted too much with his already flamboyant suit, and they hindered Jones in his

"EVEN AS THE OLD GODS HAVE EXPERIENCED SEVERE DECLINE IN WORSHIP, HE'S STILL AT THE HEIGHT OF HIS POWER. ANANSI IS ALL ABOUT BEING AT THE FOREFRONT OF THAT WAR."

: ORLANDO JONES :

performance. Mr. Nancy's hair, the colors he wears, his pocket watch, his pocketknife, his hat—everything was put together so that he would have a host of things to touch and move as he talks. "Mr. Nancy is a spider," Jones explains, "so I wanted the full use of my hands, as an allusion to the eight tentacles. He's very busy with his hands—how he uses his fingers is a big part of the character."

In his monologue to Mr. Wednesday and Shadow, Mr. Nancy stops fidgeting only when he reaches his conclusion: "Angry gets shit done." In that moment, he is all voice and power, but until then, all the clothes, the hair, and the style remind the audience that he's a spider, a god, and a trickster.

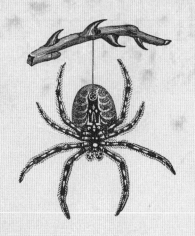

He was looking at Mr. Nancy, an old black man with a pencil moustache, in his check sports jacket and his lemon-yellow gloves, riding a carousel lion as it rose and lowered, high in the air; and, at the same time, in the same place, he saw a jeweled spider as high as a horse, its eyes an emerald nebula, strutting, staring down at him; and simultaneously he was looking at an extraordinarily tall man with teak-colored skin and three sets of arms, wearing a flowing ostrich-feather headdress, his face painted with red stripes, riding an irritated golden lion, two of his six hands holding on tightly to the beast's mane; and he was also seeing a young black boy, dressed in rags, his left foot all swollen and crawling with black flies; and last of all, and behind all these things, Shadow was looking at a tiny brown spider, hiding under a withered ochre leaf.

—American Gods, *chapter 6*

The MYTHOLOGY of ANANSI

Sometimes a spider, sometimes a man, Anansi traces his roots back to the Ashanti people of present-day Ghana, who regard him as the spirit of all knowledge and stories. Passed down through oral tradition, his folklore traveled from the West Indies to Sierra Leone, Curaçao, Aruba, and more, ultimately landing on the shores of the Caribbean and the New World along with ships full of slaves. In America, he was regarded as a symbol of slave resistance, surviving through his cunning and trickery. His stories also kept alive a link to the past in Africa as slaves passed his stories down through generations, providing a sense of identity and community.

Anansi also shares similarities with Br'er Rabbit, who originated from the folklore of the Bantu-speaking peoples of South and Central Africa. Another passenger on the slave ships from Africa, Br'er Rabbit's tales are similar stories of a small and vulnerable creature surviving by his wits and cunning. Jones recalls this association as a part of his childhood. "I'm from the southern United States," he explains. "My great-grandparents and grandparents spoke about Anansi and Br'er Rabbit as African folktale characters."

"Angry is good.
Angry gets shit done."

—MR. NANCY, EPISODE 8

MR. JACQUEL & MR. IBIS

MR. JACQUEL [AKA ANUBIS] and Mr. Ibis (aka Thoth) are brothers of sorts, though like the Zorya sisters and Czernobog, they are not related by blood. Predating every other god by centuries, they are mythological contemporaries, both hailing from ancient Egypt as far back as 3100 B.C.E. Thoth, the Egyptian god of writing and wisdom, is a scribe of the past, delving into our stories to find out who we are. Anubis, the god of the afterlife, is the judge that we all must meet to discover our fate after death. Together in the mortal world of *American Gods*, they are the proprietors of Ibis and Jacquel's Funeral Parlor, which they have run for many generations. It's a handy occupation for a pair of gods so intimately involved with the stories, bodies, and souls we leave behind.

They share a close bond, understanding each other's moods and idiosyncrasies as only the closest family members can. Ibis is excitable, while Jacquel is much more serious. For instance, in episode 4, after Laura comes back to life, but before she is brought to the funeral parlor to have her decaying flesh put back together, Jacquel chats about her with Ibis. As Jacquel preps another body for burial, he can tell that Ibis is itching to start a new story. "Ibis is very excited about Laura," explains actor Chris Obi, who plays Mr. Jacquel, "because she inspires another story, something that gives him purpose." Jacquel shoos Ibis away from the mortuary to go tell his tale, which ends up being about Essie Tregowan, or Mad Sweeney's *Coming to America* interlude.

As with the other Old Gods, Anubis and Thoth have experienced a decline. Thoth feels it less, perhaps, because he draws his power from the stories he weaves and needs less external validation. Anubis, though, is aware of his need for devotion. His role as a psychopomp, a guide to the afterlife, is essential, but he has mostly been relegated to the dusty corners of history books and museums. Indeed, Obi sees a link between being an actor and playing a god. "As an actor, you have to connect," he explains. "You have to find a way in. The problem for these gods is that they are dependent on people believing in them. It's like acting. You have your moment where people go 'Wow!' and you depend on that."

IBIS THE GUIDE

IN MANY WAYS, Mr. Ibis is our guide to the gods in the series, for he is the one who narrates many of the *Coming to America* vignettes. While Jacquel attends to the recently deceased, Ibis retreats to his study with pen and ink. From that study come his tales, and these stories are woven throughout *American Gods*.

"I love the sense of mystery that surrounds Ibis," extols actor Demore Barnes, who plays Mr. Ibis. "I got a sense from the text, and from talking to Bryan and Michael, that he relishes withholding little bits and pieces of information. I play him as one who is always holding a secret, and I think in fact he is."

This mystery belies a deep knowledge, appropriate for an ancient god once worshipped as the source of all language, wisdom, and even thought itself. Ibis is keenly aware of where everyone comes from: their circumstances in life, motivations, flaws, past weaknesses. He's aware of everyone and everything. There is no surprising Ibis, not even when Laura is yanked back into mortal life from the precipice of the afterworld, something that shocks Jacquel.

Ibis is a man of many words, and his manner of speaking is as integral to his character as his costume or mannerisms. Barnes worked to perfect the lyrical quality of his voice, adopting the cadence of a storyteller who wants to transport the listener to another land. "There's a great relish that he takes in the text,"

Barnes explains. "He's almost chewing the words, delighting in their pronunciation and meaning. He's boldfacing, italicizing, and underlining as he speaks. It's fun and theatrical without, I hope, coming across as melodramatic."

ANUBIS AND LAURA

MR. JACQUEL CARRIES himself with a deep sense of history and gravitas, appropriate for his role. He also seems weary, as anyone might be after doing the same job for the past five thousand years. Then comes Laura, who ends up in his domain not because she believes in Egyptian mythology, as in the case of Mrs. Fadil (in episode 3), but because, unbeknownst to Laura, she has been killed by a god. This is no ordinary death, and so no ordinary god will see her through to the afterlife.

As Anubis discovers in their encounter in episode 4, Laura is much more than meets the eye. Impetuous and stubborn, she's not only pissed that she's dead, she's obstinate in the face of Anubis's authority. When he reaches for her heart, she slaps his hand away, assuring him that it is, in fact, heavier than a feather. This ruffles his feathers, to say the least. Then, in the blink of an eye, she is gone, leaving the unflappable Anubis with his chin on the floor. His worst fears have been realized. A soul meant to be ushered off to its fate and forgotten has slipped from his grasp, back to mortal life. "Laura's perfect

"THE IDEA THAT THE GODS AREN'T BEING WORSHIPPED ANYMORE HAS A HUGE IMPACT ON ANUBIS. HE TAKES HIS JOB VERY SERIOUSLY AND IS CONCERNED ABOUT WHO WILL TAKE HIS PLACE IF HE'S GONE. SO THERE WAS ALWAYS SOMETHING QUITE HEAVY AND DIVINE WHEN I WAS PLAYING HIM."

: CHRIS OBI :

for Anubis," Obi explains. "She becomes more than just another body he's taking to the afterlife. She has a story to fulfill. Though he is certain that when she is done, once we discover why she is still walking this earth, she will have to meet her maker."

Anubis has a new sense of purpose once Laura returns to life. He must see her through her journey so that he can complete his task. This is not a loose end that he can leave dangling. When Jacquel brings Laura back to his mortuary for a makeover, he displays a heightened sense of purpose and care about his work, almost as if he were tending to a lover. "There's something very sexy about death," Obi explains. "Telling someone if they are going to paradise is a visceral power. His relationship with her becomes sensual."

DRESSING THE GODS

COSTUME DESIGNER SUTTIRAT Larlarb delved into the mythology of all the gods on the show, researching how she might bring elements of their origins into their costumes. Some characters posed a challenge because descriptions of them and their mythology were thin. Not Thoth and Anubis, who presented the opposite problem. Whole books have been written about them, and their related artifacts are displayed in museums around the world. For them, Larlarb had to pare down and be selective, finding ways to suggest their mythological alter egos without turning them into full-blown jackal- and ibis-headed gods.

Anubis was interesting for Larlarb because, in his first scenes with Mrs. Fadil and Laura, he is shown in his godlike form. Only in the later funeral parlor scenes does he appear in his mortal guise. So Larlarb worked backward, imagining his more grand and impressive form first, and then stripping it down to earth. "He's the only god that we see in his full power before we see the 'There's a god in Walmart' version," Larlarb explains. "When we finally see him in his more recognizable street-clothing version, he has elements from that godlike form in his costume, which is something that I didn't have the opportunity to do with the other characters."

For Jacquel's various costumes, Larlarb looked to Egyptian art and explored revered details in Egyptian clothing, especially among wealthy individuals of status. Anubis's tunic was a particular challenge. "There's a group of pleated tunics found in ancient Egypt that have survived for thousands of years," she explains. "It's a mystery how these pleats have stayed intact, since they didn't have the technology back then to chemically treat fabric." Today, the best fabric for this kind of pleating is a particular silk-and-hemp blend, but it was hard to find—and Larlarb ultimately had to source it from Japan. Larlarb adds, "In the end, we needed an inordinate amount of yardage to accommodate the pleating." This detail was carried over to Jacquel's street clothing. The back of his coat is finely pleated in a gray wool silk fabric, similar to the pleats of his god tunic.

In ancient Egyptian manuscripts and carvings, Thoth is depicted as a bird-headed god, often standing next to Anubis as he weighs the heart of the recently deceased on his scale. For modern-day Ibis in *American Gods*, Larlarb used his Old World, gentlemanly style to draw a connection to his mythological origins. For example, if you look closely, you'll see that the lining of his coat and his pocket square have ibis feathers on them, and his shoes feature a scaly ibis-like skin, which was painted on.

"Do you know what a psychopomp is? . . . It's a fancy term for an escort. . . . We all have so many functions, so many ways of existing. In my own vision of myself, I am a scholar who lives quietly, and pens his little tales, and dreams about a past that may or may not ever have existed. And that is true, as far as it goes. But I am also, in one of my capacities, like so many of the people you have chosen to associate with, a psychopomp. I escort the living to the world of the dead."

— *Mr. Ibis*, American Gods, *chapter 16*

The MYTHOLOGY of ANUBIS and THOTH

In early Egyptian civilizations, the dead were buried in shallow graves, which was a boon to roaming jackals and wild dogs, who dug them up to dine on the freshly deceased human flesh. Adopting this scourge as a source of strength, Anubis was conceived, a jackal-headed god who guarded the cemeteries and the souls they contained. His role evolved over the next millennia, and he became the god of embalming, a psychopomp, and Guardian of the Scales. In *The Book of the Dead*, Anubis, under the watchful eye of Thoth, is seen measuring a human heart against the weight of an ostrich feather, which represents truth. Souls heavier than the feather would meet their end in the belly of Ammit, the devourer of the dead. Souls lighter than the feather would pass through to heaven and immortality.

Meanwhile, Thoth is the ibis-headed Egyptian god who penned the heavens into existence. Without his words, the Egyptians believed, the gods would not exist. With a power to rival Ra, the sun god, Thoth invented writing and alphabets, acted as arbiter between the forces of good and evil, and invented a host of scholarly disciplines, including science, religion, philosophy, and magic. Thoth paired with Anubis as a psychopomp, recording the lives and deeds of the dead and their final judgment on the scales. Barnes was impressed by the god's broad power when he delved into the mythological roots of his character. "When I was doing my research, I had a clear sense of his omniscience," Barnes explains. "He's seen as the inventor of language itself, which is quite profound and powerful. We have a unique ability as humans to formulate a particular idea and express that idea. But to even think the thought, we need the words for it. I found it remarkable that Ibis, in some ways, holds the key to thinking itself, to imagination, to ideas, let alone the expression of them."

"Death is not a debate."

—anubis, episode 4

Bilquis

Though the Queen of Sheba, another name for Bilquis, was not technically a god, she is included in the pantheon of *American Gods* as a goddess of pleasure and creation, returning men and women to their point of origin through her particular brand of all-consuming sex.

Her backstory in the *Coming to America* vignette at the beginning of season 1's final episode is in some ways a history of the rise and fall of female power. Worshipped in ancient times as the queen of sex and pleasure, Bilquis has been pushing men's buttons for thousands of years. Her story shows how men have challenged her again and again, wanting to dominate this powerful woman. As men's weapons have gotten stronger, and she has been pushed out of her kingdom into the wider world, her power has slowly dissipated, until she becomes homeless on the streets of LA in the time of ISIS, watching their armies destroy her ancient temple in Yemen on a restaurant's TV.

The backstory provided fertile ground for the costume, makeup, and sets departments, which were tasked with researching and developing material for a range of eras, from the ancient Barbar Temple of Bahrain to 1970s Tehran to present-day Los Angeles. That latter setting, when Bilquis has reached the lowest point of her journey, reduced to living and begging on the mean streets of Hollywood, was a challenge for Colin Penman, the head of makeup, who was tasked with creating a suitably downtrodden visage for her character. "Trying to make Yetide look ugly—like the life force has been drained from her—is one of the hardest things I had to do on the show," he recalls, speaking of Yetide Badaki, the actress cast as Bilquis. "The quality of her skin is such that no matter what you do to it, when the lights go on, it all vanishes. I had to resort to gluing pieces on her face to give her some sort of nondescript disease."

Rory Cheyne, the production designer, was particularly excited about the nightclub set in 1970s Tehran. "There was amazing stuff in Iran in the seventies," he comments. "I researched this Frank Lloyd Wright building in Tehran called the Pearl Palace. It was this crazy building with circular ramps and staircases and a giant fountain. People say it's either one of Frank Lloyd Wright's worst or one of his best projects ever. I looked at that building as a starting point for the disco design."

This story prefaces an episode that sees an unleashing of feminine power in the form of Easter. Bilquis adds a layer to this story line, showing another goddess who, through an ill-advised alliance with the New Gods, is coming back into her power.

"Once upon a time, there was a fucking Queen. She had it all. The glory, the power, worshippers eager to give and grateful to receive. Why? Because she had the gift of the gift, the blessing of the blessing. Hers to bestow. And her place of worship, well, that was the place to be—that was the goddamn shit."

—Mr. Nancy, episode 8

BILQUIS

> "AMERICA, TOO, CAN TAKE ISSUE WITH A WOMAN OF POWER. IT FINDS WAYS OF CUTTING HER DOWN. OF PUNISHING HER FOR HER DARING TO BE."
>
> —MR. NANCY, EPISODE 8

OF THE CHARACTERS THAT appear only briefly in the book, Bilquis is the most memorable, and for good reason. It's hard to excise the image of her consuming a lover through her vagina as he worships her in delirious ecstasy. It's a sex scene with more layers than an onion, and co-showrunners Bryan Fuller and Michael Green were excited to unpack it. They worked with visual and practical effects to create what they called "the vagina nebula," a rendition of the cosmos to which Bilquis's lovers are delivered, a kind of blissful preconscious state, after being sucked up into her body.

In the book, this scene appears in the first chapter, and it sets the reader's expectations for the novel's tone. The message Gaiman seems to be sending is: *Here's a scene of an ancient goddess eating a man with her vagina. If you can handle it, great. If not, then maybe this isn't the book for you.* For the same reason, Gaiman and the showrunners decided to include it in the first episode of the series. Between Bilquis and the Vikings' *Coming to America* vignette, the first episode is by far the most violent and sexual, letting viewers know to expect some extreme material in the episodes to come.

"Bilquis is an LA woman for most of the show: Streamlined modern meets oversized baroque. I designed her apartment set, with its voluptuous curves, to match her status as goddess. We see very few belongings, as she is all about sensation, one intensification on top of another. The color of liver and velvet and taffeta-pleated drapery surround her, with an oversized deco fireplace as her headboard."
—*Patti Podesta, production designer*

The success of the scene relied heavily on the VFX depart-ment, who had to tackle one of the longest VFX sequences in the show. "I remember spending a couple hours in a coffee shop in Toronto trying to nail down what we wanted it to look like once we went inside the vagina nebula," recalls VFX supervisor Kevin Tod Haug. "It starts in the car with Mr. Wednesday. He blows the spores off a dandelion out the window, which we fol-low up into the sky where we eventually see Bilquis's lover float-ing in space with his digital erection. We turn around to see what he's grinning at and it's this anatomically correct vagina nebula that we fly into and then come out in Bilquis's room. I think the whole thing is, honest to God, five minutes long. And most of it is CG. It's a big deal to be doing that on TV."

As for Bilquis, in the book she returns only briefly and is killed, in a terrifying way, by Technical Boy. Yet Green and Fuller wanted to expand her role for the series. She is more than one iconic scene. She represents an interesting nexus between the Old and New Gods, which they saw as an important layer to the story. An Old God who hails from biblical times, she never-theless has come to depend on the New Gods for the technol-ogy that has lifted her from the gutter and restored a semblance of her former glory. The series explores this dichotomy, adding Bilquis to the list of female characters made more substantial by the showrunners.

FINDING BILQUIS

CASTING BILQUIS WAS an interesting process. For the auditions, casting directors Margery Simkin and Orly Sitowitz decided to use the iconic sex scene, since that was the bar that any actress would eventually have to meet. It made for some interesting conversations with the agents, who had to be told that the character's major attribute is "vagina-eating." Simkin and Sitowitz saw over a hundred auditions for the part and were impressed with the level of openness and commitment from all the women, but Yetide Badaki had something special. "She was so free," Sitowitz recalls. "She got Bilquis right away, and it was clear that nudity and the physicality wouldn't be a problem. She's fantastic."

Badaki brings a natural sensuality and physical power to the role. She takes what could be played as a trumped-up sex worker and finds layers of meaning in her sexual con-quests and struggle to find connection. The deeper Badaki dug into the character, the more points of connection she found. "It's becoming harder and harder to find interper-sonal relationships," Badaki comments. "People are afraid of not living up to their image on social media. Not actually meeting up with people because they want them to have that image in their head. Bilquis brought up all of those issues of connection for me."

DATE OR DIE

UNLIKE YOUR AVERAGE person on the dating scene, if Bilquis doesn't constantly replenish her source of physical and emotional worship and connection, she loses her power. Unfortunately, the conquests that she finds in the modern age pale in comparison to the devotion she experienced in her ancient heyday. "The connections Bilquis finds don't come with the proper nutrition, so to speak," Badaki explains. "She's surviving on these dalliances, but they're nothing compared to the passion of the worship and connection she felt in eras past. I like to compare it to living on greens and vegetables and food from the earth or subsisting on crap. You can live, but it's different. The hunger is still there."

This void is the perfect opening for Technical Boy to step in, offering her technology, a new dating app, to improve the volume of her conquests, if not the quality. With few options left, she acquiesces. As her circumstances improve, she comes to view Technical Boy as a necessary evil. She is a survivor, and though she doesn't like the feeling that he is controlling her, she is watching and biding her time. Technical Boy is uncomfortable with her sensuality and feminine powers, preferring to keep her at arm's length, which means that he doesn't realize the threat she may eventually pose to his authority.

WORSHIP ME

BILQUIS DOES NOT just take from her worshippers. She gives something back as she consumes them. In the world of *American Gods*, the gods are created by the energy and power of people's beliefs, be it in a deity or a device. Badaki recognizes that this transaction doesn't just give the god power, it empowers the worshipper as well. If you can create a god through your own belief, then how powerful are you? "In that moment, when worship is at its peak," Badaki explains, "that's part of the gift that she gives. She reveals the god in her partner, and she is worshipping them as much as they are worshipping her. She is welcoming them back into that greater cosmos and creativity."

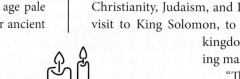

> "BILQUIS SEES HER RELATIONSHIP WITH TECHNICAL BOY AS A NECESSARY EVIL. SHE IS A SURVIVOR AND WILL FIND A WAY TO PUSH FORWARD THROUGH TECHNICAL BOY AND HIS TECHNOLOGY, SINCE IT'S HOW SHE CAN REACH MORE 'WORSHIPPERS,' OR AT LEAST THE HAPPY MEAL EQUIVALENT. IT ALLOWS HER TO CONTINUE EXISTING UNTIL SHE CAN FIND SOMETHING BETTER."

: YETIDE BADAKI :

When doing research, Badaki did not find much written about Bilquis. The Queen of Sheba is a historical, if somewhat legendary, figure, not a goddess, though mention of her can be found in the writings of three major world religions. Christianity, Judaism, and Islam all include the story of her visit to King Solomon, to whom she journeyed from her kingdom in modern-day Yemen, bearing many gifts.

"There isn't a lot of specific information about Bilquis," Badaki explains. "She's referred to as the Queen of Sheba and is found in texts from many different cultures. However, they refer to one incident, and from that you get that she was a woman of great wealth and intelligence, and was widely admired."

Badaki found more insight into Bilquis's relationship with her worshippers from research that she did into ancient fertility goddesses. "One goddess who really influenced me was Oshun from Nigerian myth," Badaki explains. "She enjoys being in her skin and sometimes possesses people. First she feels ecstasy and joy, and then sadness because she can't give them the full joy that she experiences." Bilquis tries to fulfill that promise of returned love and joy, delivering her conquests to a state of bliss. But there is still an emptiness that follows that she can't ignore, leaving her satiated but not satisfied. Just as most humans crave a connection that goes beyond sex, Bilquis seems to be searching for a partner whom she can keep rather than consume. For instance, we learn in her *Coming to America* backstory that at one point she meets one such woman in Tehran in the 1970s, but this mortal love eventually dies of AIDS in America.

Badaki's sensitivity to Bilquis's character and motivations paid off with her audience. "A lot of women have reached out to tell me how Bilquis has resonated with them," she comments. "They find the idea of her fascinating and empowering. There are a lot of myths that talk about the act of lovemaking and the center of orgasm as an endless source of creation and creativity. It almost feels like a welcoming home."

"For Bilquis and her temple, we created the starry night and atmosphere alongside a dramatic CG liquid dance by her suitor, who himself is taken over by the black liquid. We first established the best shine and texture for the liquid, then applied the animation to time with the actor's dance movements, ultimately reaching Bilquis."

—*Bernice Howes, VFX producer*

A GODDESS IN MODERN DRESS

WHEN CREATING THE costumes for Bilquis, costume designer Suttirat Larlarb was inspired by an image in a book that she has owned since the 1980s, a monograph of costume designer Eiko Ishioka. It's a photograph of a woman in a red dress seemingly standing in the eye of a hurricane. "Everyone responded to that interpretation of Bilquis," Larlarb explains. "I kept going back to it as a jumping-off point. If Bilquis were a woman walking down the street in LA, what would she wear? No matter the era, her clothes needed to have a goddess-like drape to them."

As Bilquis is seen through the centuries, her clothes and jewelry were chosen by Larlarb to reflect the appropriate culture and time period, as well as various interpretations of Bilquis and the Queen of Sheba. Prints may have a Middle Eastern sensibility, and nothing is modern or overly structured. "Every color, every shape was thought out and deeply researched," Badaki elaborates. "We had conversations about how Bilquis could wear something contemporary, but with a detail that seems out of time. The red dress in the beginning is something you could wear now, but it also seems from another era. The outfit she wears in the museum is very fifties starlet, like something she would have held on to or that would draw her eye because it's what she recognizes."

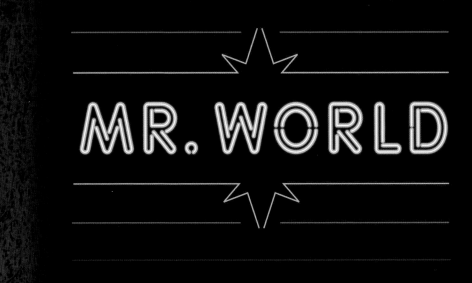

MR. WORLD

"I GET IT. I DO. YOU'RE AN INDIVIDUALIST. RUGGED. INDIVIDUALS. IT SIMPLY DOESN'T WORK ANYMORE. BRANDS, SURE, A USEFUL HEURISTIC. BUT ULTIMATELY EVERYTHING IS ALL SYSTEMS. INTERLACED. A SINGLE PRODUCT. MANUFACTURED BY A SINGLE COMPANY. FOR A SINGLE GLOBAL MARKET. SPICY, MEDIUM, OR CHUNKY, THEY GET A CHOICE OF COURSE, *OF COURSE*. BUT THEY ARE BUYING SALSA." —MR. WORLD, EPISODE 5

MR. WORLD IS NOT what he seems, though who he really is, is a mystery at the heart of *American Gods*. He appears first as the leader of the New Gods, though anyone who has read the novel knows that there are many more layers to his character. He offers a master class in deception, having duped both the New and Old Gods to believe in him, his powers, and his intent. "All we really know for certain about him is that he is a dangerously endowed individual," executive producer Michael Green elaborates. "If he is indeed an individual. He seems to know everything about everyone. He seems to worship a collective, and he makes a frightening amount of sense, if you're willing to listen."

Not everyone is open to Mr. World's point of view, however, especially the Old Gods, who have no interest in joining the world of technological domination that he pitches. They are gods of long-established habit, much like a stereotypical grandparent trying to understand Snapchat or Tinder. There is a lack of connection between the world that Mr. World envisions and the world that the Old Gods want to bring back. For instance, in episode 5, Mr. World arranges for the arrests of Mr. Wednesday and Shadow after the bank robbery so that he can have them brought to the local police station, where he makes his pitch to woo them over to the side of the New Gods. But Wednesday refuses to listen. Listening is dangerous because, as Wednesday says, "People are comforted by knowing answers to things." It helps people sleep at night to think that they've already answered the big questions. And Mr. World has a very new take on what it is to be a god in this rapidly changing modern world.

This conversation is our first in-person introduction to Mr. World. The showrunners explored a range of ideas on how to set the scene for the encounter. They were tempted to evoke the power and flamboyance of the gods with something Bond-like—a castle in Los Angeles or shooting skeet with a peacock feather in their hats. But Mr. World is so strange—and Crispin Glover, the actor who plays him, brings such an innate otherworldliness to the character—that they ultimately settled on the plainest set they could conceive: an interrogation room at a police station. "We wanted their meeting to be in a room that is so banal that Mr. World would seem like a unicorn brushing his teeth," Green explains.

Though it provided the perfect setting for Mr. World's entrance, the small interrogation room posed a unique set of challenges for the episode's director, Vincenzo Natali. The script has five charismatic and strong-willed characters coming into conflict in a room not much bigger than a walk-in closet. "It's a crazy scene," Natali comments. "Everyone is in their own reality. Media is doing her thing, and Tech Boy is doing his thing. As I recall, the script is about nine pages long. And we're in a very small room. It was a challenge to make it more than a series of talking heads. Turning the walls into a giant video screen was one way I could think of putting the scene into another gear and giving some kind of visual relief. In the end, there's so much surrealistic craziness going on that I think it works."

> **"IT WAS IMPORTANT TO BRYAN AND MICHAEL THAT WE GET A SENSE OF MR. WORLD HAVING A MORE SOPHISTICATED 'GODFLESH' TREATMENT— BOTH TO DIFFERENTIATE HIM FROM THE OTHER GODS AND TO SUGGEST WORLD AS A QUALITATIVELY GREATER THREAT. TO HELP ACHIEVE THIS, CRISPIN DELIVERED HIS LINES IN MULTIPLE ORIENTATIONS TO THE CAMERA, WHICH GAVE US THE OPPORTUNITY TO CREATE HIS TEMPORARY MULTI-HEADED FORM."**
>
> : JEREMY BALL :
> VFX SUPERVISOR

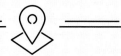

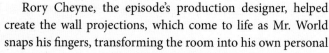

Rory Cheyne, the episode's production designer, helped create the wall projections, which come to life as Mr. World snaps his fingers, transforming the room into his own personal PowerPoint presentation. "We built our real set and then we built the same dimensions out of projection screens," Cheyne explains. "We'd never done projection at that scale before, and it worked out well. I remember I was down on set looking at the monitors and I was talking to Darran Tiernan, one of the three cinematographers on season 1, and I asked, 'So when are you going to move over to the projection set?' And he responded, 'We're in the projection set.' And I couldn't tell the difference."

AN AMERICAN GOD

CASTING MR. WORLD turned out to be much easier than Bryan Fuller and Michael Green anticipated. They wrote their version of the character with a certain voice in mind, thinking of someone like Crispin Glover, someone with his same charming, forceful, unusual, and captivating delivery, who could be both human and otherworldly at the same time. But they didn't think they would be able to actually get Glover for the role. When it came time to talk about casting possibilities, Fuller and Green used Glover as a reference, but they couldn't think of many others who could bring his level of craft and presence. Luckily, they didn't need to. One day later, casting directors Margery Simkin and Orly Sitowitz emailed, writing, "Hey, you're having coffee with Crispin Glover tomorrow morning."

The timing, it seemed, worked perfectly for Glover. When Bryan and Michael met him in person, their encounter might as well have been written for the screen. Green says, "We were excited because we are fans of everything he's done: music, acting, his wonderful and specific directing. It was a very, very warm day—I was sitting there sweating and gross. I look out the window over Bryan's shoulder and I see Glover coming. We watched this gentleman out of another era in a three-piece velvet suit ride up on his bicycle, wearing a fedora, which he took off as he stepped into the restaurant. Just as a matter of course, as one was taught to do back in the days of black-and-white film."

The showrunners were prepared to pitch the series idea, though they knew that it was difficult to sum up. They had yet to find their elevator pitch for *American Gods*, one that succinctly captured its many ideas, vignettes, characters, and

"There is an art of persuasion that is important to the character of Mr. World."
—Crispin Glover

themes. Up to then, discussing the project was always something of a process and not easily grasped; some people had responded with confusion or a promise to read the book to gain more clarity. In Hollywood, drawn-out explanations run the risk of losing the audience. Glover, on the other hand, sat patiently through their ten-minute explanation of the show; then he smiled and said, "I understand. That sounds great." It was not lip service. Green says, "The show is in a plane of existence that is familiar to him. My suspicion, with complete affection, is that he lives his life with a degree of uncompromised magic."

The casting was a match from the start. Glover proved himself to be just as unique, polite, and genteel as Mr. World, though thankfully without any of the character's menace and manipulation. "I don't know anyone who can make bonkers so gentle, so elegant," Green comments. "The role is bizarre, and his performance is a very controlled version of strange, but he has an elegance to him that is very much a choice."

Natali was thrilled to be able to work with Glover. "I'm a huge fan of his work," he comments. "I grew up doing Crispin Glover impressions. I could really hear his voice in the script. How Mr. World appears on-screen was entirely his creation—I had to do very little except point the camera at him. I think it's really important when you're introducing Mr. World to do it with a little bit of flourish. The way Glover makes his entrance is almost Michael Jackson-esque."

THE PERFECT SUIT

DRESSING MR. WORLD was all about the details. He wears a suit in the show, as he does in the book, but for such a mysterious and powerful character, it couldn't be just any off-the-rack pinstripe. It needed to be as precise and imposing as the god it contains. "We wanted him to be impeccable, to wear something that might be described as the platonic form of a suit," costume designer Suttirat Larlarb recalls. "All the details needed to be perfect, the angles sharp, with no visible curved lines. Even the pocket square was like a shard. We ended up using a piece of folded white patent leather instead of a sloppy, beautiful silk sort of thing. It was futuristic in the art school sense of the word. Like futurism as opposed to *Star Trek*."

The fedora that Mr. World wears was directly inspired by Green and Fuller's first meeting with Glover. At first he did not want to wear it, but Green was able to convince him otherwise. In the back of his mind, Green knew that he was trying to re-create for the audience that thrill he had upon first glimpsing the actor ride up on his bike, of watching a gentleman walk into a room and redefine it simply by his manner and dress. Glover had made a three-piece velvet suit and a fedora on a hot LA summer day seem normal. In *American Gods*, Mr. World appears in a Midwest police station, dressed to the nines, and infuses formality with his particular brand of menace.

"The animation of the rainbow unicorn and the teddy bears and gummy bears coming out of the rockets was developed between Michael Green, Bryan, and me trying to figure out how crazy we wanted it to be. They just said, "Go as far as you want and we'll take a look at it."
—*Rory Cheyne, production designer*

Jesus

The *Coming to America* that prefaces episode 6, "A Murder of Gods," examines the arrival of the Mexican Jesus as he helps a band of immigrants enter the United States across the Rio Grande. This ragtag group of men, women, and children, all crossing the border illegally in the dead of night, are met by a vigilante border militia who open fire on them as they come ashore. Both sides display evidence of their Christian faith—the gun-wielding militia man carries a cross on a chain attached to his gun while the immigrants openly thank Jesus as they touch American soil for the first time. And both are breaking the law and invoking their faith in the process (though only one is breaking a commandment, it must be noted). Which is the true faith? If belief makes it so, what side will Jesus come down on?

In this case, the answer is clear. Jesus is Mexican, blending in with the immigrants and helping them reach the far shore. When the militia men start firing, he sacrifices himself to save the immigrants, in true Jesus style. "We wanted to get inside the emotional experience of the immigrants—to humanize them," Adam Kane, the episode's director and an executive producer, comments. "Part of this was filming the scene in a way that conveyed the underlying religious message. The symbolic visuals that we include are based in classical Christianity. When our Jesus character is on shore after he saves a drowning man, we imbue a halo behind his hair with the glowing headlights of a truck. When the militia men start firing and he puts his hands up to protect the family that's trying to run to safety, he's shot through the hands where Jesus was nailed to the cross. Those are the kinds of specific images that Bryan and Michael write into the material. That's part of the fabric of executing their vision of the series."

This *Coming to America* vignette is both more political and more personal than the others in the first season. "What is our humanity when it comes to embracing immigrants who are coming to our home?" Kane asks when discussing the political implications of the scene. "Here the viewer gets to know families, women, and children who are trying to make their way into America, we presume for a better life from where they came. As we see these souls cross into America and reach their goal and be so grateful to be where they are, they're mercilessly gunned down. I think you're left with the question of why. Because of fear? Because of some sort of archaic idea that outsiders are going to threaten our way of life?"

The latter, personal perspective was a surprise to Kane, but added a layer of poignancy to the shoot and the resulting footage. "One of our extras in the scene," Kane explains, "the person who plays the older man who crawls onto shore and kisses the ground and thanks the heavens—as a young child he actually made that journey. So for him, it was very emotional. Especially since the place where we shot, even though it was outside of Toronto, at night it really resembled the border between Texas and Mexico."

> "You've got your white Jesuit-style Jesus, your black African Jesus, your Mexican Jesus, and your swarthy Greek Jesus."
>
> —Wednesday, episode 3

EASTER
AND THE
JESUSES

> "PRAISE THE LORDS. PLEASE HELP YOURSELF AND THOSE LESS FORTUNATE TO THE BUFFET. I'VE GOT PLENTY OF HONEY HAM."
>
> —EASTER, EPISODE 8

IN THE BOOK *AMERICAN* Gods, Easter appears only briefly, though she has an important role to play in Shadow's fate. We meet her first in San Francisco's Dolores Park, where she flirts with him as Wednesday tries to persuade her to join his war between the gods. Her relationship, and dependency, on Jesus comes up in their conversation, but her own pagan history goes largely unmentioned. Her powers of resurrection aren't revealed until she is called to help Shadow as he lies dying on the World Tree.

Executive producers Bryan Fuller and Michael Green knew that Easter's character was rich for expansion. She's a classic case of a woman underestimated by her peers. Thus, in the TV series, Easter goes through a transformation in the final episode worthy of the season she represents.

THE EASTER COMPROMISE

IN EPISODE 8, Shadow and Wednesday arrive at Easter's mansion on Easter Sunday, and as they drive up, their car is swarmed by a herd of rabbits, one of the most recognizable symbols of Easter, in what seems to be a feeble attempt to stop their progress. Wednesday ignores them, to the likely demise of a few of the fluffy bunnies. Yet an endless supply of rabbits seems to spill out over the entire estate, which is decked to the nines for Easter's big day. Or is it Jesus's big day? As much as this is Easter's house and it's decorated in the pastels of spring with treats and rabbits (some cooked, some alive), the majority of the guests are the big man himself. Jesus appears in numerous guises, which represent the wide range of cultures that worship him. It's his party, it turns out. Easter is just the hostess.

Easter is all smiles and courtesy, but beneath the surface she is a housewife trapped in a marriage she never really wanted. Like Bilquis, she is dependent on a constant supply of modern media to get by. She has become an adjunct to Jesus's religion so that people will speak the name Easter at least once a year. But existing under the guise of the Christian holiday is something older.

Jesus is well-to-do now, but Easter remembers when he was a new idea, a plucky upstart messing with the status quo. Before Jesus came along, she was Ostara, the goddess of spring, and she had legions of worshippers who paid tribute to her and the season that she brought forth each year. Then, during her sacred month of April—or Ostermonat, as it was known in Germanic culture, from which she hails—Jesus's resurrection occurred, and Easter was faced with a choice. If she joined with him in celebration, sharing her name, eggs, rabbits, and powers of resurrection, she could ride his ascending coattails to world-wide popularity. Or she could follow the path of her pagan brethren and be relegated to the dustbins of mythology. She chose the former, which benefited her greatly, but not without personal sacrifice. "Easter aligns herself with people who are going to help her cause," explains actress Kristin Chenoweth, who plays Easter. "Because the truth is, she wants the earth, the animals, her plantation, and her luck to remain the same."

"On the surface, Jesus and Easter get on very well," Green agrees. "They are like peanut butter and jelly as far as America is concerned. But that wasn't always the case. When the

> "THE BUNNIES ARE HER MINIONS, AND I THINK WE'LL FIND OUT THAT SOME OF HER BUNNIES MIGHT HAVE MORE POWER THAN HER. SHE GETS HER DIRECTION IN ONE SCENE FROM A BUNNY; IT SPEAKS TO HER. WE'LL FIND OUT WHO THAT PARTICULAR BUNNY IS, I'M SURE, IN SEASON 2."
>
> : KRISTIN CHENOWETH :

candy-coated shell around her cracks, Easter lets slip that the compromise she had to make is not one she particularly likes."

RABBITS COME HOME TO ROOST

AT HER CORE, Easter is a pagan goddess with largely forgotten powers. But even a dormant power can still shape the person who wields it. As Kristin Chenoweth muses: "When you use magic or prayer for good, that's wonderful. But I think Easter lets things come in that are darker. That's the fun in playing her."

Easter manages to balance the complexities and contradictions of her world until Mr. Wednesday comes along. Easter is the ultimate hostess, so she welcomes him with an invitation to stay and feast, but she knows that Wednesday is a manipulator and has come to disrupt her life. Wednesday picks at the scab of her self-delusion, pointing out that by making a deal with Jesus she has become a shadow of her former self. Wednesday makes public Easter's inner conflict, and this prompts "Jesus prime" (as the showrunners refer to the main Jesus in the episode) to say with great sincerity and sadness, "I feel terrible about this." It's a simple line that captures the complexity of their relationship. "Jesus believes he was doing her a favor," Green elaborates. "And in her WASPy way, she may have made him feel that everything was okay."

THE JESUS DOZEN

HOW MANY JESUSES are there in the world? In episode 3, Wednesday says, "You've got your white Jesuit-style Jesus, your black African Jesus, your Mexican Jesus, and your swarthy Greek Jesus." But at Easter's mansion, we see just how many Jesuses there are.

Fans of the novel may be surprised to see Jesus at all. He is conspicuously absent from the book, despite being the most popular religious figure in America. Originally, when he was writing the novel, Neil Gaiman sketched out scenes involving Jesus and other deities or figures from three of the world's major religions—Christianity, Judaism, and Islam—but in the end he decided not to include them. Gaiman reasoned that the deities associated with the big three were doing very well, so the turf wars being kicked up between the Old and New Gods would

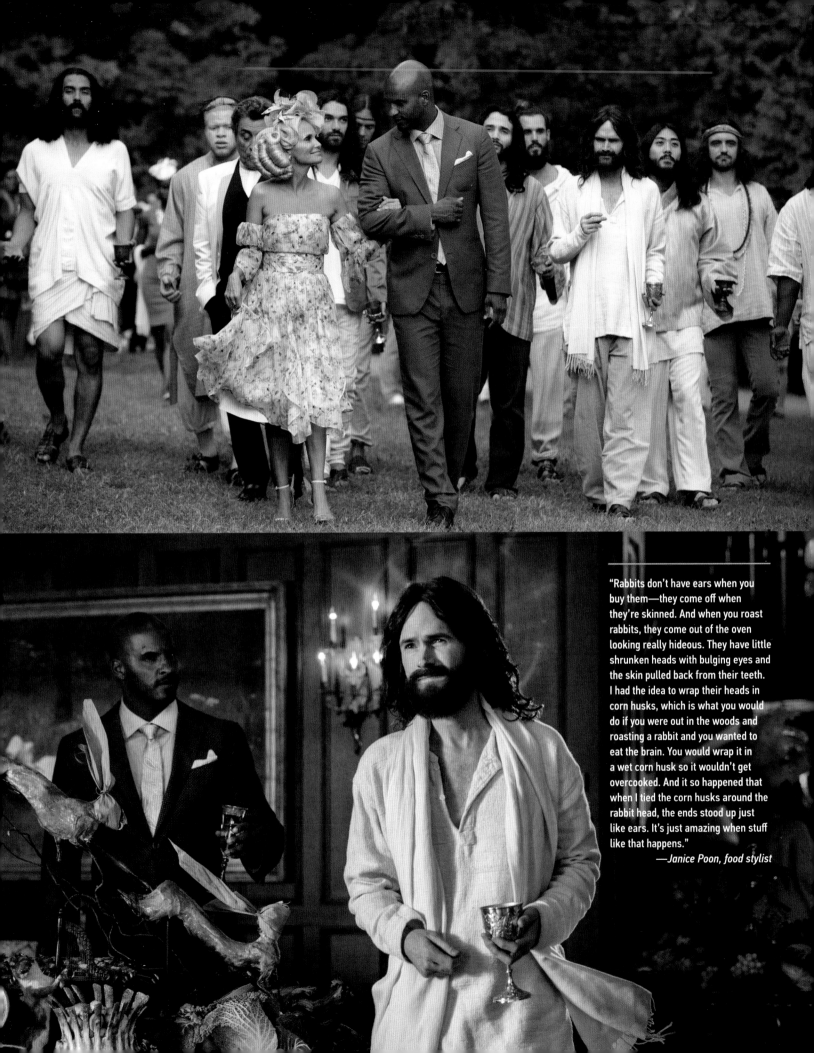

"Rabbits don't have ears when you buy them—they come off when they're skinned. And when you roast rabbits, they come out of the oven looking really hideous. They have little shrunken heads with bulging eyes and the skin pulled back from their teeth. I had the idea to wrap their heads in corn husks, which is what you would do if you were out in the woods and roasting a rabbit and you wanted to eat the brain. You would wrap it in a wet corn husk so it wouldn't get overcooked. And it so happened that when I tied the corn husks around the rabbit head, the ends stood up just like ears. It's just amazing when stuff like that happens."
—*Janice Poon, food stylist*

pass beneath their notice. As they developed the TV series, Green and Fuller saw that they could delve deeper into the major religious faiths in America. "Approaching *American Gods* as a show, we knew that we were going to have more real estate," Green explains. "We had an opportunity to say something about faith in America, specifically about the role of Jesus."

But who is Jesus? Or rather, which version of Jesus would they represent on-screen? Throughout history and around the world, Christianity includes many sects and expressions, and Jesus is presented in many different ways. In the end, the showrunners decided to include them all and to create a great big Jesus party at Easter's house. This is meant to honor the diversity of the Christian faith, not to present it as a polytheistic religion—the Jesuses are all expressions of the same divine person. Thus, one Jesus is dressed as a West Coast hippie, while another hails from Mexico; another is from Africa, while one wears the ornate regalia of the Russian Orthodox church.

Fuller and Green took special care when it came to writing Jesus. Specifically, as a dramatic character within the world of *American Gods*, they felt that Jesus's success may have made him blind to the concerns or problems of other deities. Jesus does not have to concern himself with the competition between the Old and New Gods, so he doesn't notice that Easter, his partner on this day of celebration, has been disguising an open wound since the day of his resurrection. "We imagined Jesus to be the most sincere and likable god we would come across," Green elaborates. "We meet so many asshole gods along the way in *American Gods*. But Jesus is love, faith, and belief incarnate. He has the best of intentions, which is extremely endearing."

EASTER FINEST

IN THE SEASON'S final episode, Easter wears only one outfit, so costume designer Suttirat Larlarb wanted it to be everything you might associate with Easter. Her dress touches on the world of the Old Gods—it drapes with a classic, romantic line—but in its kitschy overabundance of pastels, flowers, and butterflies, which cover her from head to toe, it also evokes her relationship with Media.

Larlarb drew inspiration from the episode's setting. "Something that often gets ignored in television and film is how the setting relates to the characters," she explains. "So you end up having a show set in Alabama, but the cast is dressed like they're in New York or LA." In the book, Easter's scene is set in San Francisco, which would have required different clothing—if only to account for the weather, since in San Francisco the fog might roll in at any moment and plunge the temperature by twenty degrees. In the series, Easter's mansion is in what might be Long Island or rural Connecticut. To play up the idea of a classic Easter parade celebration on a warm, East Coast spring day, they decided to create a pastel nightmare. "Easter teeters on the brink of crass," Larlarb explains. "But Chenoweth could never be suffocated by anything you put on her. She has this amazing presence. In the fittings I would show her a timid, safe version of the dress next to the exploded, ridiculous version. She always went for the boldest direction."

Colin Penman, head of makeup, drew inspiration from Larlarb's work on the dress for his approach to Easter's look. Knowing that Easter would be playing against Laura, the dead wife, there was also an opportunity to show the contrast between the two of them. "Against Laura Moon's pallor, we wanted to make Easter just that—very Eastery," he explains. "I took inspiration from her wardrobe and her headpiece, which had all these great, springlike colors. We wanted her to glow, so almost all the products I used on her had shimmer to them, so that she showed as much life as we could put in her."

Easter's look is used for dramatic effect in the episode's final scene. Summoning her latent, primal, feminine power, Easter drains the spring from the earth, taking back the life that she has given. As she casts her spell, her structured, intricate bouffant hairdo comes tumbling down, turning her from prim hostess to barefoot pagan goddess. "When things well up in her, that hair comes down," Chenoweth explains. "And then everything runs amok. The hair is gone, the dress is dropped, and she's a different person."

The Jesuses, on the other hand, took a village to dress. With dozens of Jesus costumes to develop, Larlarb deputized her

"Easter is extremely happy that people are still celebrating Easter. But she's a little pissed off that Jesus has stolen her holiday. She puts on a happy face when she has to, but there's a deep part of her that's very angry. And where is she going to put that anger?"

—*Kristin Chenoweth*

team of assistant designers. Larlarb and the episode's director, Floria Sigismondi, put together a mood board of reference images, and then they sourced as much as possible from opera and costume houses in LA, New York, and London. "It was a collage process," Larlarb explains. "We made six or seven variations of the tunic top that Jesus wears, based on the typical image of him in religion and pop culture. We tweaked it so that it felt a little more modern, but still had its roots in what everyone would see as the 'Jesus tunic.' Then we added the specific ethnic details to make a particular Jesus."

"I'm telling you . . . I'm doing fine. On my festival days they still feast on eggs and rabbits, on candy and on flesh, to represent rebirth and copulation. They wear flowers in their bonnets and they give each other flowers. They do it in my name. More and more of them every year. In my name, old wolf."

—Easter, *American Gods*, chapter 11

⚞ The MYTHOLOGY of OSTARA ⚟

The chocolate bunnies and plastic eggs that line the aisles of American grocery stores in the weeks before Easter have nothing to do with Christianity. They are the domain of Ostara, or Ēostre, the goddess of spring worshipped by pagan Anglo-Saxons. The exact origins of the Easter bunny are unclear, but both the bunny and other Easter traditions like dyeing eggs likely came over to America along with German immigrants of the 1700s.

Ostara is associated with the dawn, fertility, and the rebirth of spring. Worshippers, the ancestors of those intrepid German immigrants, would light giant bonfires in her honor and play games involving eggs and bunnies (as well as eating the same at feast time). Christianity handily dovetailed with this pagan holiday, keeping certain attributes while adding Christ's resurrection as the holiday's raison d'être. ❧

"There's power in the sacrifice of a god."

—WEDNESDAY, EPISODE 7

Notes From the Set

Ian McShane

Do you believe?

First day on the film set. We are actually going to do this.

"We're going to put back your call by half a day."

"Why?"

"The cat with the large balls isn't behaving very well and we're behind."

Hurry up and wait. The mantra of the film business.

"Neil, Michael, Bryan, Ricky, and Ian can we get some photos, never know when will have you all on the same set at the same time and we're still waiting for the special cloud effects rig outside the plane windows to be fully operational."

"Of course."

They pay me to wait; I do the acting for free. Outside the studio, it's 105°. I can't wait to do the exteriors in the cashmere coat, but it defines Mr. Wednesday and is a nod to Gaiman, albeit in a different color.

Do you believe?

Oklahoma is very, very flat and very, very hot. Why have we driven what seems like a thousand miles to be in the same location we started in, and why is Ricky doing coin tricks? Christ it's hot! But at least I didn't have to film in that lockdown penitentiary or that snake-infested mesa. On the thousand mile drive back to the hotel we eat at a Sonic—the 50s revisited.

And then we are back in Toronto and it's getting even hotter. The set is closed for the day for the Bilquis introduction sequence. I hope they can do some of that in post-production or there may be an investigation into missing actors in Canada. One actor has already gone missing but for different reasons.

Meanwhile, Ricky and I are in Betty, Mr. Wednesday's Cadillac, rehearsing sweating and grumbling. As actors do.

Do you believe?

We are in an alley way in Hamilton in a wind tunnel with a snow machine. It's 110° and I'm still in the coat. Old Gods, New Gods, fantastic actors all, come and go. Days turn into night, nights into day. In the studio, it's always night.

Rewrites and re-shoots (can't do everything in post). Press visits, publicity shoots. How many more episodes? Was I born in Toronto? And then suddenly it's over.

Do you believe?

I go into the studio for the dialogue synch.

"Would you like to see some of it?"

"No, I trust you guys."

Do I? I have to.

Four months later: SXSW Festival, Austin, Texas. First showing and it's on the big screen. It's starting.

Do you believe?

One hour later as the credits roll: I do now, and I loved every minute of it.

Location scouting image, with a stand-in for
Shadow discovering the carousel.

Talking Season Two with Neil Gaiman

SLADAR
SA 1
SB 1
SC 1
SD 1
SCENE VX103B   TAKE 1
D4
EP
201

Mr. Wednesday and his wolf.

In conversation with Emily Haynes

IN MARCH OF 2018 I had the privilege of chatting with Neil Gaiman about season two of *American Gods*. The series is going into the new season with a new showrunner, Jesse Alexander, at the helm, an expanded cast of gods and mortals, and an exciting slate of elaborate sets and locations, including the carousel from House on the Rock. Changes are coming, as Neil hints in his musing about the story and characters in the works, though fans can expect to spend ample time with Shadow, Wednesday, and the rest of the gang.

Is season two going to be more faithful to the novel?

NEIL: No. But it's going to run along similar tracks. It will do the same thing that season one did where the characters might do things that cause the story on the screen to ramify in different directions. But we can point to the book and go, "Okay, this occurs between this point in the book and this point in the book."

Are there storylines in season one that you think won't carry forward into season two?

The Hall of Gods

Shadow on Odin's beach

Everything will carry forward in ways that feel appropriate to *American Gods*. There were ideas that we played with which we're now thinking, "Okay, well, we won't be doing that, then." An example would be the Media and Easter friendship and love. I don't know if that's going to happen. It was something we were going to do, but it depended on Gillian. Now I don't know if that's going to happen. We will see. We only had Gillian for the show's first season, which is great because it means we had Gillian being Old Media. She was a Lucille Ball/David Bowie/Judy Garland/Marilyn Monroe–era of Media, and that's an era that already feels as much ancient history as some of the old gods do. The idea that we can now bring in a New Media is delightful.

Have you cast the actor to play Media in season two?

We haven't yet cast our new Media, but I'm very much hoping for somebody younger, quite possibly somebody of color. Probably still female. We'll get to find out some fun stuff in the new season. What's the relationship that this Media is going to have with our Technical Boy? It's time for new Media.

Inside Odin's Hall

Khali, a Hindu goddess with many hands that hold knives, swords, and severed heads

I'd love to talk about House on the Rock. We got a glimpse of it at the end of season one, or at least the road to House on the Rock. Is that going to be the centerpiece of season two?

I'll put it this way: we are definitely visiting House on the Rock. I think the visit to House on the Rock is going to be more like the one in the novel, which will mean one visit. Stuff will happen. It will be fun and exciting, and there will be the gods in the carousel. So the answer is yes, of course we're going to House on the Rock, because how could you not? This is part of the story. And getting the balance of what happens at House on the Rock is going to be really interesting.

Do you think that we're going to run into some of the other characters from the book that we haven't seen yet, like Sam Black Crow, or Mama-ji?

Oh, yeah. Jesse Alexander wrote the first draft of episode one. I wrote the second draft. Jesse's now writing the third draft, and I'm sure we will toss it backwards and forwards until it shoots. Mama-ji is definitely in there. I'm hoping that we'll run into Sam Black Crow by episode three or four. Casting her is going to be really interesting. We need to find a fantastic Native American actress. I'm sure there are many of them out there, but finding her is going to be an adventure.

Mr. Wednesday's wolf and the magic of special effects.

Mr. Wednesday's wolf transformation.

Is the format going to stay the same, with the "Coming to America" vignettes prefacing the episodes?

Occasionally. The idea that the show has both "Coming to Americas" and "Somewhere in Americas" was intentional and runs all the way through. We never set out when we were creating American Gods to preface every single episode with a "Coming to America." We will continue to add them as they work.

What are you the most excited about for season two?

I think I'm most excited about watching our actors going back to their characters now that they know who they are. In season one, they got to find themselves. Seeing Ricky going back and being Shadow again. Seeing Ian being Wednesday, seeing Emily being Laura. That's the excitement for me.

AMERICAN GODS
WOLF TRANSFORMATION SCALE

5' 7.5"

TRANSFORMED WOLF (150% LARGER)

5' 7.5"

TRANSFORMED WOLF (50% LARGER)

5' 7.5"

TRANSFORMED WOLF (25% LARGER)

5' 7.5"

CAROUSEL WOLF

Odin and others emerge from a quasar.